Child Care Revisited

D0294352

Child Care Revisited:
The Children's Departments
1948-1971

How the child care specialists of the past
hold lessons for the future

Bob Holman

ICSE

Institute of Childcare
and Social Education UK

Published by the Institute of Childcare and Social Education UK
c/o Integrated Care Limited, 57 Graham Road, London W4 5DR

Copyright © Bob Holman 1998

The right of Bob Holman to be identified as author of this work has been asserted by him
in accordance with the *Copyright Designs and Patents Act 1988.*

Design and typesetting by Blade Communications 01926 882176
Printed by Stephens & George Limited
ISBN 1 871872 50 2

Contents

Foreword

As the senior manager of a specialized child care resource that provides services for some of the UK's most troubled and, therefore, challenging youngsters, I am acutely aware of the need for constant assessment of child care delivery throughout the country.

As the Prospects Organisation provides a nationally available service we deal continually with agencies from various areas. This broad contact has identified two factors that remain clearly evident. First, there are many hard working and child-centred professionals with the field. However, they appear to harbour a substantial amount of concern that 'Things are not going as well as would be desired.' Many things influence this unease, including a concern in relation to the current structuring and generic responsibilities spread across Social Services Departments.

We at the Prospects Organisation are pleased to be able to sponsor Bob Holman's *Child Care Revisited: The Children's Departments 1948-1971*. The publication provides a unique opportunity to consider future plans by looking, through the eyes of those involved, at past events. To know where we are going we must know where we have been. Research and comment of this kind can be a useful tool for those with the responsibility of assessing and directing the future of child care in the UK.

Specialized services supervised by specialized departments may be a valuable methodology for raising the standards and delivery of child care and children's services. It is also useful to note that this publication will also stand as a documentation of a key historical era in the development of children's services. This alone makes it a valuable addition to social care publications.

The Prospects Organisation is a not-for-profit voluntary organisation providing registered and approved residential and fostering services for severely problematic and challenging children and young people. We specialize in intervention for youngsters who have previously experienced considerable placement breakdown.

Steve Hyland, April 1998

For further information about the Prospects Organisation contact:

Steve Hyland
Managing Director, The Prospects Organisation,
Linden House, Broad Street, SOMERTON,
Somerset TA11 7ND
Tel: 01458 274446 and Fax: 01458 274440

About the Author

Bob Holman started as a child care officer in a Children's Department. He then spent ten years in academic life finishing as Professor of Social Administration at the University of Bath. Leaving the ivory tower, he initiated a community project on the Southdown estate where he lived for eleven years. In 1987, he moved to Easterhouse in Glasgow where he works as a volunteer with a project called FARE. He writes for *The Guardian* and his recent books include *Children and Crime* (Lion Publishing, 1995); *The Corporate Parent, Manchester Children's Department 1948-1971* (National Institute for Social Work, 1996); *FARE Dealing: Neighbourhood involvement in a housing scheme* (Community Development Foundation, 1997); and *Towards Equality: A Christian Manifesto* (SPCK, 1997). He is visiting professor at the Centre for the Child and Society, University of Glasgow.

Acknowledgements

The author offers his thanks to the Barrow Cadbury Fund and the Prospects Organisation for sponsoring the publication of the book. In addition, the publication of the *Child Care Revisited: The Children's Departments 1948-1971* owes much to the goodwill of Tim Woodward and the editorial skills of Edwina Kinch. I would also like to thank the good offices of Integrated Care Ltd for helping with the distribution.

One

The Making of the Children's Departments

The 1948 Children Act receives little attention in the history books of modern times. Fraser (1973) mentions it once, while Thane (1982) gives it just two paragraphs. Today, it appears that even social work students learn little about it. Yet the Act was a radical one, for it created a new local authority service whose sole responsibility was for children, to use the parlance of the time, "deprived of a normal home life". The Children's Departments were reorganized out of existence by legislation in 1968 and 1970. None the less, in their short life-span they achieved much and the fiftieth anniversary of their establishment occurs in 1998. This book is an attempt to record some of the experiences of the Children's Departments in the words of children's officers, to evaluate their achievements, and to draw out some implications for the future of child care.

The Children's Departments can not be understood without some knowledge of how deprived children were cared for before 1948 and without some understanding of the forces that brought about the 1948 Children Act. This opening chapter will briefly trace events which led to the making of the Children's Departments. It will then outline the main events which occurred during the years of the Children's Departments as a background to the succeeding chapters.

Child Care before the Second World War
In western societies, church bodies have long provided some shelter for children without adults to look after them. As the power of the church declined so other voluntary bodies established institutions often with donations and bequests from entrepreneurs who had grown rich from Britain's expanding trade and industries. For example, in 1653, the Mancunian merchant, Humphrey Chetham, left £7,000 for an establishment known as Chetham's Hospital to provide boarding for the boys of honest, poor men. It was not just voluntary bodies. The Poor Law Relief Act (1601) instructed local parishes to accept responsibility for destitute children and added that, when of age, they should be set to work.

The Nineteenth Century
The nineteenth century witnessed significant developments in child care. A rapid increase in population, a drift to towns where over-crowded living conditions stimulated ill-heath and death, and severe unemployment all contributed to many children living in abject poverty, being left without parents or living rough. Simultaneously, the explosion of manufacturing industry meant that many citizens had money which could be given to voluntary societies. Dr Barnardo's, the National

Children's Homes and Orphanage, the Waifs and Strays Society, Muller's Homes and Quarrier's Homes are among the large institutions set-up for needy children. A visitor to George Muller's Homes in Bristol recalled that he addressed 1,150 orphans (Calman, 1875). At the time of its founder's death in 1905, Dr Barnardo's was maintaining 11,277 children. In addition to these famous bodies, there were hundreds of smaller and less well-known ones. For instance, in Fulham the Home for Fatherless Boys was started by Sydney Black so that they would not have to find "their refuge, most hated and most feared, in the workhouse" (Ainsworth, 1911, p. 82). Black's reference to the workhouse is a reminder that the Poor Law was still active. Its local administration had been taken over by elected Boards of Guardians and by the end of the century the Poor Law catered for 58,000 children in workhouses, children's homes and residential schools while a further 8,000 were boarded out with foster parents.

Stagnation With Promise

At Dr Barnardo's funeral the streets were lined with thousands of mourners. He and the other child care pioneers had made deprived children a matter of national concern. Thereafter, public concern went into decline in the early decades of the twentieth century. To be sure, the great voluntaries still maintained over a thousand children's homes. Yet, a number of the large organizations were in financial difficulties, while much of their drive and vision had been lost. In her moving account of her childhood years in Aberlour Orphanage, Dorothy Haynes pays tribute to the dedicated staff. Yet she had to endure a regimented regime with 500 other inmates and, even in the 1930s, she was forbidden to spend the holidays with her father (1973). It was not that innovation was completely missing. One society, for instance, made small grants to encourage unmarried mothers to retain the care of their babies. The voluntaries had stagnated but there were glimpses of promise.

A similar judgement could be made about the Poor Law. The growth of working class political activity resulted in some Labour politicians winning election as Poor Law guardians. Typical was George Lansbury — later the leader of the Labour Party — who was a guardian in the east end of London. From the inside he strove to humanize the workhouse and succeeded in greatly improving conditions in its children's residential school. From the outside, he campaigned for the abolition of the Poor Law and published a stirring pamphlet entitled *Smash the Workhouse* (Holman, 1990, p. 55). The campaigns were successful in that legislation in 1929 and 1930 did result in the functions of the Poor Law being handed over to local authorities where they were often implemented through their Public Assistance Departments. But it was still regarded as the Poor Law and, in the 1940s, I can recall my grandmother pleading, "Don't let me finish in the Union (the Poor Law)."

More promising child care developments occurred elsewhere. In 1909, the London County Council's Education Authority established children's care committees in which staff organized volunteers to visit families where their children's schooling was being adversely affected by poverty, ill-health and delinquency. A quarter of other education authorities followed suit. The growing child care expertise of education officials probably influenced the shape of the seminal Children and Young Persons Act (1933). The act widened the reasons for which children could be brought before the courts in need of care and protection and extended the duties of local authorities. Local authority Education Departments soon found themselves responsible for "fit person orders" under which neglected and delinquent children could be entrusted to public care. The departments responded by promoting fostering and residential establishments including remand homes.

Within central government, the Home Office oversaw the penal system which included juvenile offenders and approved schools. It set up its own Children's Branch within which progressive inspectors like Charles Russell, Arthur Norris and John Gittins argued for more humane and personal treatment for delinquents. Their impact must not be exaggerated — for instance, birching continued in approved schools — but they became an avenue through which the new academic discipline of psychology was discussed. Noticeably, Cyril Burt's classic *The Young Delinquent* was published in 1925. Similarly, psychiatry and psychology were informing child guidance clinics which spread from the USA to Britain in the 1930s. The prevailing belief within the clinics was that the children's problems of delinquency, truancy, uncontrollable behaviour and so on had to be understood by focusing on emotional causes. Some of their staff like psychiatrist John Bowlby and social workers Sybil Clement Brown and Lucy Fildes were later to be prominent child care figures.

Position in 1939
Despite the promising glimmers, there seemed little prospective of large-scale improvements in the system of child care at the end of the 1930s. The majority of children, whose parents could not cope with them, were in institutions, often large and regimented ones, staffed by untrained personnel who were not equipped to give them personal affection. The child care system was fragmented and uncoordinated. Destitute children were still the responsibility of Public Assistance Departments which remained under Poor Law legislation. Delinquent children and those in need of protection were likely to be in the care of Education Departments and needy, sick children to be looked after by Health Departments but neither of these local authority departments regarded these children as their main concern. Deprived children and other delinquent ones were likely to be in the hands of the voluntary societies. The defects of this system were not a matter of national attention. Even if they had been, the prospects of reform were slim given that the government of the day was committed to retrenchment not increased public expenditure. Then came the war.

Warfare and Child Care

As Professor Richard Titmuss (1950) has documented in his official history, the second world war stimulated a host of welfare reforms. Working-class children benefited almost immediately from the provision of welfare foods and the greater availability of school meals. Later they gained from the provision of family allowances and the National Health Service. In addition, the war was to promote a greater understanding of deprived children. This concern owed much to the experience of evacuation.

The Evacuation

During the war, the fear of bombing impelled the government to evacuate millions of children. I was one of those small youngsters who, in September 1939, stood at a railway station with a gasmask and a label with our name on it bound for an unknown destination. Priority was given to those in heavily populated urban areas and hence many children from low-income families and poor housing were moved to the countryside. As I have explained elsewhere, the evacuees initially met complaints from their foster parents about their lice, bed-wetting and lack of manners (Holman, 1995). But, once the blitz started, the complaints turned to sympathy.

The evacuation profoundly influenced the care of children separated from their parents in these ways.

First, it pushed local authorities into taking more action on their behalf. The councils who received children had to find foster homes and arrange medical and educational services for them. Later, over 500 hostels, or children's homes, were established for children who could not fit into foster homes. Much of the finance came from central government, so councillors and officials became accustomed to cooperating closely with government departments in the provision of child care.

Second, it increased the number of child care practitioners. After initial reliance on volunteers, some local authorities appointed officials to find and supervise foster homes — or billets as they were often called. Residential staff had to be found for the hostels. Dorothy Watkins had been a governess, youth club leader and a welfare worker abroad. During the war, the Labour Exchange advised her to apply for the post of billeting inspector with the Welsh Board of Health. She was appointed and so inspected the fostering work being carried out by local authorities. At first hand, she observed the growth of a child care occupation (Watkins, 1993).

Third, evacuation stimulated an interest in the methodology of child care. Susan Issacs (1941) and her colleagues studied the experiences of evacuees in order to ascertain what made for successful fosterings. Donald Winnicott and Clare Britton (1947) were involved with hostels and wrote about the role of residential care and the skills needed by their staff.

Fourth, it put the needs of separated children back on the national agenda. As the psychiatrist, Donald Winnicott (1957), pointed out in one of his popular broadcasts, almost every family in Britain had a child evacuated or was looking after evacuees. It was in the interests of all to understand how separation affected children and how to deal with it. Further, the government began to consider what should happen after the war to evacuees who had no home to which to return. An informal committee at the Ministry of Health acknowledged that they should not go into the care of Public Assistance Departments with their stigma of the Poor Law. Other departments joined in to moot the possibility of a new local children's committees (Parker, 1983). Of course, in these years the government was planning many other welfare reforms. The cause of child care required another push. It came in the person of Lady Allen.

Lady Allen
Marjorie Allen was the widow of a Labour peer. During the war she used her political connections to expand nursery education. Then, as she tells in her autobiography (1975), while visiting a school she noticed a group of listless children. They were from a voluntary children's home and, after visiting several, she launched a vigorous campaign to improve them. She was not alone and, under the guidance of other prominent figures, the campaign widened to call for a review of the lot of all deprived children. On 15 July 1944, Lady Allen had published in *The Times* a now famous letter in which she complained that, "many thousands of these children are being brought up under repressive conditions". The response was amazing. *The Times* received more letters about deprived children than any other single subject during the war. The government had to respond and in December the Home Secretary, Herbert Morrison, announced his attention to set up a committee of inquiry.

The 1948 Children's Act

The Monckton Report
Perhaps, because so much legislation was being formulated, and because he was preoccupied in bringing the evacuees home, Morrison seemed in no hurry to announce the members of the committee. Matters came tragically to a head in January, 1945 concerning a child, Dennis O'Neill, who had been committed to the care of Newport Borough Council whose education officers, unable to find a place in Newport, put him in an isolated farm in Shropshire. There he was brutally murdered by his foster father. Sir James Monckton was appointed to examine the tragedy. He swiftly reported in May and attributed blame to inadequate supervision of the foster home by the two councils. This fault sprang from the use of unqualified staff and a breakdown in communication between welfare agencies. He recommended the introduction of a new official, the children's officer, with a personal concern and responsibility for deprived children. The report (1945) added weight to Lady Allen's plea for a unified system of child care.

The Clyde and Curtis Committees

Even before appointing Monckton, the Home Secretary had named the members of two committees.

To enquire into existing methods of providing for children who, from loss of parents or from any other cause whatsoever, are deprived of a normal home life with their parents or relatives; and to consider what further measures should be taken to ensure that these children are brought up under conditions best calculated to compensate them for the lack of parental care.

One committee, chaired by Myra Curtis and including Sybil Cement Brown and Lucy Fildes, was for England and Wales. The other, under James Clyde and including the novelist Naomi Mitchison and Dr Nora Wattie, was for Scotland. The committees reported in 1946 and their main recommendations can be summed up as follows:

- Central responsibility for deprived children to be with one government department.

- At local authority level, a single committee, the children's committee, should be established for deprived children.

- The new committee to appoint an executive officer, the children's officer, to provide what the Curtis Committee called "a personal element". (para 441)

- With adoption not applicable to many children — as they still had ties with natural parents — boarding out (fostering) was considered the best form of care for most children. The Clyde Committee argued that fostering was the nearest approximation to family life in which the child "secures the necessary opportunity to build up his (stet) own personality and equip itself for the transition to independence and self-reliance". (para 45)

- The disadvantages of institutional life to be minimized by reducing the size of homes.

- Training to be considered necessary for both child care visitors (later called child care officers) and residential staff.

The reports were received with general acclaim. The response was more muted in Scotland where there had been no Dennis O'Neill and no Lady Allen. None the less, most commentators agreed with the leader in *The Times* of 16 October, 1946 which urged legislation to follow based on the reports'

fundamental plea for a concentration of the direction of policy in one department at the centre, and of its execution in the local authority, acting through a special committee and a single specialist officer.

MPs of all political parties gave backing to what became the 1948 Children Act which legislated for many of the recommendations. In particular, it stipulated that local authorities were to create children's committees with a duty to receive into care, children under the age of 17 whose parents were unable to provide for them and whose welfare required it. The committees also took on duties in regard to children committed by the courts, for protecting private foster children and for supervising adoptions.

The 1948 Children Act unified a fragmented child care system and placed responsibility on a single local authority committee which, through its Children's Departments, had no other duties save those in regard to children "deprived of a normal home life". Voluntary societies were to continue but children in their care were to be visited "from time to time" by the local authority. At central government level, the Home Office in England and Wales and the Home Department in Scotland took control. Jean Packman suggests that they received the responsibility because their inspectors were considered more efficient than those of other ministries (1975, pp. 7-8). The care of children, as never before, was in the hands of statutory bodies. But it was not just a new organizational structure, for the Act carried a philosophy about children. Jean Heywood, in her classic *Children in Care*, says,

> in a clause, perhaps unmatched for its humanity in all our legislation, the Act defines the general duty of the local authority towards the child in care, 'Where a child is in the care of a local authority it shall be the duty of that authority to exercise their power with respect to him so as to further his best interests, and to afford him opportunity for the proper development of his character and abilities.' The measure of the long road the reformers have travelled can best be seen by placing beside this clause the definition of the poor law to such children as it still remained until its dissolution in 1948, modelled on the words of the Elizabethan statute, 'To set to work or put out as apprentices all children whose parents are not, in the opinion of the Council, able to keep them.' (1959, p. 158)

Significantly, the 1948 Children Act became law on the same day as the 1948 National Assistance Act which opened with the memorable words, "the existing poor law shall cease to have effect."

The Children's Officers

The Children Act stipulated that local authorities should appoint a new official, called the children's officer who was to have responsibility for children in care (section 41). When the bill was going through parliament, the Home Secretary, Chuter Ede, said, "in the future much happiness would be created and many promising lives preserved through the skill, affection and attention of those officers" (cited by Packman, 1975, pp. 9-10). Who were the first children's officers? Kenneth Brill, later a children's officer himself, made an analysis of appointments by the 128 counties and county boroughs in England and 17 in Wales. Women outnumbered men by a ratio of 2:1. The former tended to have social work experience — with evacuees, as psychiatric social workers, almoners etc. They were also more likely than the men to have university degrees. The latter often had experience in local government with 34 coming from posts in education departments (Brill, 1991). Mention has already been made of Dorothy Watkins who had worked with children at home and abroad as well as in the evacuation before becoming the children's officer for Cornwall. Ann Medley had discontinued medical training to join the Women's Army Corps in the war, first driving trucks as a private soldier until demobilized as an officer. She then became the children's officer for Gloucestershire. Ian Brown had been taken into the workhouse as a child and was eventually boarded out with his grandmother: although academically bright, the Poor Law authorities would not pay for him to stay on at school and he joined the education service as a junior clerk. He worked his way up to assistant education officer in Manchester from which position he was appointed the city's children's officer.

Whatever their different backgrounds, many of the children's officers were united in a strong desire to implement the new legislation in order to improve the lot of deprived children. In eventuality, their new departments lasted only until 1971 (1969 in Scotland). The Children's Department, for older people like myself, were created and ended in our lifetimes. I feel it is important to preserve this piece of history; partly because the achievements of its participants deserve to be remembered, and partly because they may have lessons for the child care systems of today and tomorrow.

How best to write an account of the Children's Departments? No doubt, more able people than myself will do so through a detailed examination of the documents, of the minutes of committees and reports lodged in the Home Office. I have chosen a different approach by recording what happened in the words of some of the leading participants in the Children's Departments. I have been able to interview a number of former children's officers and two former Home Office inspectors. Of course, the Children's Departments consisted of more than children's officers. Elected members of children's committees, residential staff, child care officers, administrative and clerical staff, foster parents, and, particularly, children in care and their parents, were just as much a part of the children's service. I regret that I did not have the resources or time to collect their views.

1998 is an appropriate date for a book in that it marks the 50th anniversary of the 1948 Children Act. Already a number of children's officers and child care officers have died and the remaining ones are — as my rail card puts it — senior citizens. If nothing else, this book will put into the print the words of men and women who built up and maintained the local authority Children's Departments.

Stages of the Children's Departments

In interviewing the children's officers, I did not wish to impose an agenda. Rather, I wished them to talk about the experiences and developments which seemed most important to them. Before visiting them, I wrote to explain my purpose of making a kind of oral history of the Children's Departments. I did have a number of questions in case they flagged but nearly all talked freely. Some had prepared for the interview and had looked up old papers and reports. Others just articulated whatever memories came into their mind. The interviews do show some unity amongst the children's officers as to what topics are most important. But there are differences and references to certain government reports and legislation may be confusing for readers who are not familiar with the child care history of the period. For the sake of clarity, I have constructed the main stages of child care for 1948-1971. In this I draw particularly upon Jean Packman's *The Child's Generation* (1975) and John Murphy's *British Social Services: The Scottish Dimension* (1992). The stages are as follows:

Establishing the Departments

For the initial two to three years, the children's officers had to strive to create and establish their new departments. This involved learning to work with the children's committees, the town clerks and the heads of other local authority departments. For people like Dorothy Watkins, who had no previous experience of local government, this was not easy. She tells how, on her first day, she was accommodated in a small hut in the car park and discovered that "the Children's Service was to be a section of the Clerk's Department, so that I was not on a par with other chief officers, employed by the council" (1993, p. 128). In Manchester, Ian Brown had the advantage of experience in the council and found both children's committee and other departmental heads to be accepting and cooperative (Holman, 1996).

Many children's committees in England and Wales did share the enthusiasm of the children's officers for the new Act. The same could not be said of Scotland. As John Murphy stated, "it was commonly thought that Scotland possessed the panacea to the problem in a fine system of Boarding Out and that improvements, rather than major change, was all that was required" (1992, p. 30). Thus, in order to save costs, some local authorities had suggested that "to justify the post, the children's officer should also act as clerk to the burial ground" (p. 10). Whatever the welcome and whatever the enthusiasm of the children's committees, nearly all children officers soon found themselves almost overwhelmed by pressure to take children into care. In the first 21 months, Manchester Children's Department received 1,694 children under the provisions of the new Act. At a time of a baby boom and acute shortage of housing, many of these were for short-term care while mothers were in hospital for births or illnesses and so, in the same period, a high number were soon returned home. None the less numbers in care did rise substantially. In England and Wales, the overall total in care on 30 November rose from 55,255 in 1949 to 62,691 in 1951. In Scotland from 9,068 in 1949 to 10,250 in 1952.

In those turbulent days, it was fortunate that the Home Office child care inspectorate was forging links to advise the new departments. The Home Office was also helpful in regard to the training of staff. Even before the Children Act, and following an interim recommendation of the Curtis Committee, the government had established a Central Training Council in Child Care. It promoted courses in child care at various educational establishments so that a growing number of qualified child care officers along with a smaller number of qualified residential workers began to enter the service. Some of the former were involved in the establishment of the Association of Child Care Officers (ACCO) in 1949 whose membership grew from 241 in 1950 to 845 in 1959. In Scotland, a regional branch of ACCO was inaugurated in 1954 and by 1959 had 194 members. Along with the Association of Children's Officers (ACO) and the Residential Child Care Association (RCCA), ACCO was to have an influential voice within child care circles.

Children's Homes

Having established the Children's Departments and set up mechanisms for receiving and discharging children, many children's officers turned their attention to the quality of their residential care. Many existing children's homes were large and impersonal and Jean Packman titles her relevant chapter "The Mouldering Bastions." Most departments gave attention to reducing the size of the residential units. In Manchester, the bold decision was made to close Styal Cottage Homes which accommodated over 400 children. Particular concern was felt about large residential nurseries and these were often broken down into smaller units or abolished altogether, although they persisted longer in Scotland. Between 1954 and 1970, numbers in residential nurseries in England and Wales fell by nearly 5000 to 2,500 children. But what could replace the institutions? A favourite option was family group homes. In the 1950s in Coventry, the children's officer, Mary Barnes, promoted a number of such homes, taking 6-8 children, on council estates they were headed by housemothers whose husbands went out to work. Miss Barnes reported,

> The children became part of the local community ... attended local schools and were encouraged to mix and make friends with other children on the estate (1980, p. 37).

It should be added, however, that family group homes were not without their critics. The former children's officer, Leslie Turner, in his interview for this book, said,

> I found that over a period of one or two years the membership of the 'family' completely changed. Children came and went(rehabilitation with parents was becoming more common) and so did the staff.

It was also pointed out that the job was often too demanding for just one full-time housemother and that if she left then the children did not have the continuity of other staff who remained. Some authorities also opened reception and assessment centres where staff decided just what kind of placements the children needed. These centres required particularly skilled staff but the fact was that residential establishments of all kinds had difficulties in recruiting qualified workers. The shortage continued and the Williams Report, *Caring for People*, published in 1966 found that 70 per cent of staff were without any qualification and that a third changed each year.

Fostering and Adoption

Difficulties in running residential care was one reason why, in the middle 1950s, many Children's Departments began to emphasize fostering. The 1948 Children Act had laid upon local authorities a duty to board-out children in their care unless "not practicable or desirable for the time being" (Section 13). The inclusion of this duty sprang, no doubt, from the arguments in the Curtis and Clyde Reports that foster families had more in common with natural families than institutional care.

In 1953, Dr John Bowlby reinforced the case for fostering in his popular Pelican *Child Care and the Growth of Love* which was derived from his research for the World Health Organisation, published in 1951 as *Maternal Care and Mental Health*. The case for fostering was completed on the grounds of expense. Britain was facing post-war economic difficulties with the results that the brakes were placed upon public expenditure. Local authority Children's Departments, although initially aided by 50 per cent grants from central government, had taken up more local money than had been anticipated. Fostering was held to be cheaper than children's homes. In 1952, the Home Office reinforced this duty with a circular that added "boarding-out is the least expensive method of care both in money and manpower"(1952).

In fact, research undertaken much later by Knapp and Robertson throws doubts on the cheapness of fostering but it was certainly the accepted wisdom of the time (1989). By the mid 1950s, therefore, many Children's Departments gave priority to promoting fostering. The Home Office encouraged this by publishing annual boarding-out figures which became known as the league tables in which departments compared each others' progress. According to the Curtis Report, 29 per cent of children in public care in England and Wales were boarded-out. By 1953, Children's Departments had pushed the figure up to 42 per cent with a peak of 52 per cent being reached in 1965.

In Scotland fostering was already established. In 1950, a reporter from the *Glasgow Herald* visited the Children's Department where the children's officer proudly produced a nineteenth century book to show that Glasgow had been boarding-out children since the 1770s (M. Carson, 1950). The level of boarding-out was always around 60 per cent as a result of a long tradition placing pauper children to work in outlying crofts and farms.

The proportion of children fostered in England and Wales fell after 1965 and by

1970 was back to 42 per cent. The decline stemmed from two reasons. One was the realization that fostering was not *the* answer to all children's needs with research showing that a disturbingly high number of long-term placements broke down. The other was that child care officers were having to give more of their time to preventative and other work. Significantly, section 13 of the 1948 Children Act which made fostering the preferred method to be pursued by local authorities was replaced by section 49 of the Children and Young Persons Act (1969) which gave local authorities a duty to provide accommodation and maintenance "as they think fit".

Fostering organized by local authorities must be distinguished from arrangements in which parents themselves find, place and pay private foster parents. The 1948 Children Act gave local authorities child life protection duties to supervise these placements and placed a responsibility on the foster parents to give notice when they were intending to take a child. The Children Act (1958) and the Children and Young Persons Act (1969) slightly changed the responsibilities of local authorities but research established that Children's Departments gave low priority to this work and lacked sufficient powers to supervise effectively (Holman, 1973).

The 1948 Children Act also gave local authorities considerable duties in regard to adoption. They had to supervise all children placed for adoption; be prepared to act as *guardian ad litem* for children as they came before the courts for an adoption hearing; to register voluntary bodies as adoption agencies. It also gave them the power to place for adoption children who were in their care and, after the Adoption Act (1958), they were empowered to arrange adoptions for children who were not in care. Consequently, the number arranged by Children's Departments rose from around 1,000 a year to over 3,000. A number of departments appointed adoption officers and adoption practice became a recognized part of the child care specialism.

Prevention

One of the few criticisms made of the 1948 Children Act was, in the words of Roy Parker, "that it did not deal with the question of prevention" (1983, p. 212). It certainly gave them a duty to return children to their homes, where appropriate, but it said nothing about preventing them having to come into care in the first place.

As numbers in care increased and as experts like John Bowlby began to argue that children could be emotionally harmed by removal, so the case for prevention gathered in momentum. In parliament, the Select Committee for Estimates in1951-52 declared that the cheapest way of helping deprived children was if the family crisis was "remedied before the actual break-up of the home occurs". In 1952, the Association of Children's Officers extended its list of objectives to include "to encourage and assist in the preservation of the family". In 1954, David Donnison, after studying children in the care of Manchester and Salford, found that the departments "had few resources to help parents look after their own children" (1954, p. 32).

As early as 1950, the Home Office, the Ministry of Health and the Ministry of Education issued a joint circular urging local authorities to form co-ordinating committees amongst their various departments in order to make plans for families whose children might have to come into care. Moreover, the Children and Young Persons (Amendment) Act (1952) placed a duty on local authorities to investigate any suggestion that children were in need of care and protection whether the neglect was wilful or not. Some Children's Departments did pursue preventative work and a few appointed family caseworkers to specialize in it. But doubts were expressed about the legality of spending public money on this end. Both the Association of Children's Officers and the Association of Child Care Officers urged the government to act.

In 1956, the government set up the Ingelby Committee with a brief to examine the juvenile justice system and the prevention of cruelty to children. To this it added, perhaps as a result of the lobbying, a brief to ascertain whether local authorities should be given new powers to prevent the suffering of children in their own homes. Following its report 1960, the government enacted the Children and Young Persons Act(1963). In section 1 it states,

> It shall be the duty of every local authority to make available such advice, guidance and assistance as may promote the welfare of children by diminishing the need to receive children into or keep them in care ... or to bring children before a juvenile court.

The act not only sanctioned the prevention of children entering public care but it also added the prevention of delinquency.

A number of Children's Departments took up their new role with some enthusiasm and, as Jean Heywood and Margaret Allen showed, developed innovative ways of helping families even though the child care officers were handicapped by a lack of funds (Heywood & Allen, 1971). Some departments made increased grants to voluntary bodies such as the Family Service Units and the NSPCC so that they could develop preventative work. They were helped by a gradual increase in the number of child care officers so that by 1970 the Children's Departments in England and Wales employed 3,741 officers. The Home Office, through the Central Training Council in Child Care had continued to expand training so that by the 1960s over a third of field staff were qualified.

In Scotland, too, attention was at last given to training in the 1960s. The Scottish Advisory Council on Child Care, with Baroness Elliot in the chair, published a report, *Staffing Local Authority Children's Departments*, in 1963 which demonstrated the inadequacies of staffing. Indeed, all of Scotland had a mere 97 child care officers. By 1968 the number of child care officers in Scotland had increased to 305. Only 60 of these were professionally qualified but this was an advance. The outcome of a combination of enthusiasm and training was seen in Manchester where a detailed study by myself (1996) shows that staff did succeed in preventing some children from entering care. However, overall numbers in care actually rose. The number in care in England and Wales in 1962 was 63,648. By 1968 it was 69,358. In Scotland, in 1963 it was 10,162 and in 1969 reached 10,797. A main reason for the increase was that the Children's Departments had been so successful in establishing themselves as *the* service for children and families that they attracted numerous referrals from other agencies. In Manchester, the juvenile courts committed so many children to care under fit persons orders that they constituted well over a third of all children in its care. Moreover, they were frequently delinquent and demanding youngsters who stayed long-term. Simultaneously, children were being referred for poor school attendance, for minor delinquency which had not reached court, and for home and school behavioural problems. The Children's Departments were becoming the centre for delinquent children and for family problems in general. By the end of the 1960s, a third of a million children a year were being referred to Children's Departments of whom only about 12 per cent came into care. Preventative work also grew steadily in Scotland so by 1969 Children's Departments were dealing with 12,980 families whose 40,735 children were not in care.

Young Offenders

The Children's Departments had been established to deal with what were regarded as deprived rather than delinquent children. Young offenders were likely to appear before the courts where the judiciary could place them on probation or send them to approved schools. Older delinquents could be sent to borstals. Yet, from the start, there was always an overlap. The courts could commit children to the care of local authorities under fit person orders and some of these might be delinquents or, more frequently, neglected children who had also offended. A number of Children's Departments were responsible for remand centres where children could be accommodated while awaiting court appearances or while a place at approved school was being found. Approved schools were directly accountable to the Home Office and most were independent bodies or run by the large child care societies. However, a few approved schools were tied to local authorities with the Mobberley Boys Approved School, which came under Manchester Children's Department, being a well known one. Further, the Children and Young Persons (Amendment) Act (1952) allowed Children's Departments to undertake the supervision of youngsters released from approved schools.

In her book, Jean Packman has a chapter titled "Deprived or Depraved?" In more detail than can be given here, she shows how a number of children's officers and other experts began to argue that deprived and delinquent children had much in common — families which could not cope with them — and that it made sense if they became the responsibility of the same service. The Children and Young Persons Act (1963) increased the number of offenders dealt with by Children's Departments but did not fundamentally change the system. None the less, individual children's officers did alter practice. Best known was Barbara Kahan of Oxfordshire who offered the services of her department to the courts. In particular, she wanted magistrates to try fit person orders before sending offenders to approved schools. Simultaneously, child care officers in the department began to supervise delinquent children on a voluntary basis. These initiatives did mean that more children came into the care of Oxfordshire, some into residential care, with the result that costs rose. None the less, the approach did appear to help some young people stop offending and it did reduce the number going to approved schools.

The Oxfordshire initiative, which was praised by the Home Office, reflected a national concern with juvenile crime. There followed a number of reports and white papers which discussed the causes of delinquency and the best ways of dealing with it. Consideration was given to whether juvenile courts should by replaced by more informal children's panels. In the end, the latter were not introduced in England and Wales but important legislation did come in the Children and Young Person's Act(1969). The age of criminal responsibility was raised from eight to 10 years. For offenders aged 10-14, it was the intention to replace criminal prosecution by care proceedings to be administered by local authorities. For those aged 14-17 years, prosecution remained an option. In addition, both offenders and non-offenders could be placed on supervision orders to be supervised by probation officers or local authorities. A new form of treatment, 'intermediate treatment' was introduced in which residential care could be combined with group activities while the youngsters lived at home. The powers of courts to send offenders to attendance centres, detention centres and borstals were modified. Approved school orders were abolished the courts could place youngsters on care orders but the local authorities were to decide their place of residence. Approved schools were changed to 'community schools with education' and were to be seen as one of the resources to be considered by regional councils when deciding the needs of their locality. The Act was never fully implemented for a general election brought in a Conservative government which changed a number of the provisions including not to raise the age of criminal responsibility, not to limit the powers of courts to send offenders to attendance centres, detention centres and borstals, and not to place restrictions on the prosecution of those aged 14-17. Even so, the Act greatly increased the involvement of Children's Departments with delinquents.

In Scotland, following the Kilbrandon Report, more fundamental changes occurred. Except for very serious offences, children were removed from the scope of the courts. The Social Work (Scotland) Act (1968) set up a system of Children's Hearings: a new local authority official, the reporter, was given the power and responsibility to refer both offenders and non-offenders to children's panels where lay members decided their futures. This reform was part of a much larger reorganization.

Reorganization

From the start, Children's Departments had to co-operate over certain families with other social services — health departments, welfare departments, housing departments, the probation service, the police and schools and so on. In his pioneering study, David Donnison observed so many officials visiting the same families that he recommended rationalization through "a comprehensive personal service" (1954, p. 74). This recommendation gained momentum as Children's Departments expanded the scope and nature of their work, especially in regard to prevention and involvement with young offenders. In 1970, Barbara Kahan pointed to,

> the very high, and rising, numbers of children and young persons referred for help, advice and guidance each year. In the period 1 April 1968 — 31 March 1969, this figure was 308,076 in an estimated population of 13,350,000 under 18 years of age, a rate of twenty three in every thousand in a twelve month period. These figures do not include nearly 18,000 privately placed foster children and children involved in adoption, 7,500 in approved schools and more than as many out on licence or under supervision, nor several thousand more being supervised in the community under various legal requirements. (B. Kahan in P. Townsend et al., 1970, pp. 61-2)

The Children's Departments had become, in effect, a kind of family service but one handicapped by their lack of control over such facilities as day nurseries and home helps. In 1960, the Ingelby Committee, after commenting on the limitations of co-ordinating between services, concluded, "It may be that the long-term solution will be in a reorganization of the various services concerned with the family" (para 47). From this juncture, matters proceeded differently in Scotland as against England and Wales.

In 1960 in Scotland, central responsibility for child care was transferred from the Scottish Home Department to the Scottish Education Department. John Murphy, himself a civil servant, commented, "The change proved fortunate as this department then deployed some particularly able and committed administrators, who saw the importance and the further potential of child care, and eventually nursed these through to the Social Work Act of 1968" (1992, p. 101). Senior civil servants were not the only influence. The voice of child care grew stronger in Scotland and both the Association of Scottish Children's Officers and the Scottish branch of ACCO began to discuss and then to put the case for a more unified service. The Scottish Advisory Council on Child Care set up the McBoyle Committee to consider the prevention of child neglect and, in its report of 1963, it recommended that local authorities be empowered to promote a comprehensive service. Its proposals, however, were overtaken by those of the Kilbrandon Committee, set up the Scottish Office and published in 1964 as *The Report of Children and Young Persons*. It led to the Social Work (Scotland) Act (1968) which amalgamated various local authority personal services, including the probation service, into a Social Work Department. The local authorities were given the wide-ranging general duty "to promote social welfare by making available advice, guidance and assistance on such a scale as may be appropriate for their area" (section 12). As mentioned, it also established Children's Hearings as a new way of dealing with both young offenders and non-offenders, a change which did nor occur south of the border.

Why Scotland had more radical reforms is difficult to explain. John Murphy attributes it to the high quality of the members of the Kilbrandon Committee, the influence of progressive civil servants, the Scottish links with Scandinavia where hearings systems were in operation, the paucity of juvenile courts in Scotland so that opposition to their abolition was not strong, and to the determination of Judith Hart, the Under Secretary of State for Scotland who was determined to carry through the legislation.

In England and Wales in 1965, the government appointed Frederic Seebohm to chair a committee "to consider what changes are necessary to ensure an effective family service." Its findings were published in 1968 as *The Report of the Committee on Local Authority and Allied Personal Social Services*. The arguments of the Seebohm Report were comprehensive leading to 206 recommendations. The essence, however, was that the services provided by the Children's Departments (whose services were mainly for children) and those of the Welfare Departments (mainly services for adults), along with parts of educational, child guidance, health, mental health and housing services, be amalgamated into one Social Services Department. The report did not consider changing the juvenile justice system which was soon to be subjected to the act of 1969. The ACO and ACCO were broadly in favour of the proposals although there were differing opinions as to whether reorganization should take place in stages rather than in one swoop.

A Seebohm Implementation Group campaigned on the grounds that the new service would have a wider range of resources, would facilitate communication, would be powerful enough to win more money and would enable the varying welfare occupations to merge into one, powerful British Association of Social Workers. The government ignored most of what the report said about the philosophy of the new service and the approaches to be adopted and passed the Local Authority Social Services Act (1970) which reorganized the services on the suggested lines. When it came into operation on 1 April, 1971, the Children's Departments ceased to exist.

Two

The Children's Officers

The story of the Children's Departments is best known to those chief officers who established and maintained them — the children's officers. I was able to trace eighteen former children's officers and two Home Office inspectors. They allowed me to visit them and to record interviews which lasted between one and a half to three hours. Subsequently, I typed out the recordings and edited them for the sake of continuity and brevity. I then returned them to the interviewees to amend. The outcomes are as follows:

Dennis Allen

Introduction

Born in 1919, Dennis Allen's parents separated and, at the age of six, he was sent to a private but progressive boarding school. He worked as a clerk until the war when, as a Quaker and pacifist, he refused to register as a conscientious objector and was imprisoned. While in jail he took an examination paper in delinquency to complete the London University External Social Sciences Diploma. He subsequently worked with the Pacifist Services Unit and, after the war, in an approved school. In 1951 he attended the LSE to take the child care course and then joined the London County Council (LCC) Children's Department. He was deputy Children's Officer in Hampshire 1963-1966 and Children's Officer of East Sussex 1966-1970. He was director of the East Sussex Social Services Department from 1971 until his retirement in 1981.

Interview

After training I joined the LCC Children's Department and was allocated to Area 9 where Margaret Hancock was the area children's officer. I had a caseload of 120, mainly teenage boys, spread around eight counties with many in institutions. When I protested to Margaret, she replied, "I'm terrible sorry, here's ten more." A lot of my time was spent in detective work for many of the boys knew nothing about their parents and I used to go locating parents who had not seen their child for years. I remember a boy in a special school in Surrey who had befriended a jackdaw. I had seen his mother in hospital in south London but the boy was frightened about visiting her. I got permission from the sister of the ward that he could bring his jackdaw; that made all the difference and he came with his bird which flew around the ward creating havoc but everyone accepted it and it made the visit possible. It meant that at last he faced the reality of his mother. He did not go to live with her but he visited and that made it easier to achieve separation from the school which had been his only home.

I worked long hours and fortunately my wife was very supportive. In fact, one boy came to live with us. As a baby, his mother was sent to psychiatric hospital; before the age of three, he had twelve placements. He came on my caseload when he was 11 and I tried all kinds of placements. He burnt down a boarding school. Then he went to a hostel where the staff promised to stick with him. They saw him through but he appeared in court several times and eventually came before a magistrate, Geoffrey Issacs, who had been chairman of Peper Harow School. The boy was in danger of going to borstal which would have finished him and he would have finished up as a recidivist. I explained that the objective was to get him settled and the bench accepted that he should live with me on a probation order. He stayed a year and was there when my wife died — and we had four daughters. But it was a turning point. He said later, "You did more than you needed to." When people now talk about professional training, I always go back to that, it is the commitment that matters most. He is now in his 50s. When he was 25, he wrote and said, "You'll be glad to know I now have only one mistress." Progress. He was making relationships. I would not have thought that possible in his first disintegrated state. I thank my family enormously for what they did.

I was transferred to Area 5 as a senior child care officer under Barbara Drake who was a good social worker and manager. Janie Thomas was also a senior in that team. Then back to Area 9 as area children's officer. In a way this was my most satisfying job because I was still in touch with the field work and still carried a caseload. It was a small enough unit for us all to support each other and to get an enormous amount of feedback.

I had one experience here that showed that abuse did occur although we were not looking for it. A neighbour of a foster mother reported that the foster child was being badly beaten. The child care officer would not believe it so we visited together. I said to him, "Please, let me do the interviewing, don't chip in unless I ask you". We got there and I explained why and the officer immediately chipped in, "You wouldn't do a thing like that, would you Mrs X?" He was typical of an attitude that could not confront serious problems. I had to insist that we took the boy for a drive and I reassured him that if he said he did not want to go back then we would see to it. He lifted up his shirt and showed his back covered in weals. The social worker was dismayed. He was a good, honest man but he could not face it. So I knew abuse went on and I suspected a lot was going on in the residential field but that was more difficult to uncover because insiders closed ranks. It could be physical or sexual abuse but there was also emotional abuse such as scapegoating children which damaged them.

Today child protection has become too formal. Everyone is now so terrified that it has a counterproductive effect. There is much advice and guidance but it is excessive in proportion to the amount of good it does. The older system in which child care officers took on child abuse as part of their caseload is preferable to the present system where often they are child protection workers. They need better preparation of social workers so that they are comfortable with what they are doing and not on edge and that means being able to care for and to work with people and not just the dissemination of circulars.

A major problem within the LCC was to change the bureaucracy. The biggest bone of strife was clothing. When boys were ready to leave residential care, you took them to this great warehouse and the warehouseman used to take them to the shelves and say, "You're about size 15, that should do." As for shoes, the buying manager had bought 10,000 pairs of heavy black shoes, which the kids call beetle crushers, and they all had to be used up. It was all done for bureaucratic processing not for the children and to change that and the attitudes associated with it is the most important job in the first ten years. The changes were promoted by the newly trained people and if you ended up in a department in which you were the only one you were by no means popular because you were asking people to change the habits of a lifetime In these circumstances, the Association of Child Care Officers, which put me in touch with other officers, was a great means of support.

When in London, I set up a place which was subsequently the basis of a TV series called Bachelor Father. It was a home run by a single man, who looked after the children. It was in Surrey and when its children's officer, Beryl Watson, heard about it she exploded, "You can't do this." I said, "It is alright, it's not a foster home, it is a private children's home — that was an invention, there was no such animal — but it stopped Beryl. He went on to do wonderful things with kids and set up a couple of other homes with women in charge. He invited me back on the 25th anniversary when the now grown-up kids and their wives were there. It was a risky thing because Peter could have turned out a bad egg but the LCC approved it. When it was made into a TV programme, they could not imagine how we could have been so stupid as to place children with a single man. The producer and the main actor, Ian Carmichael, asked how we knew he was not a paedophile. We had to explain that we took safeguards but in the end we took a risk because the children who went there had been in many other institutions and the chance of a good placement was worth it.

In 1963, I went to Hampshire as deputy children's officer. Amicia Carroll was the children's officer, a somewhat patrician lady in the mould of the original Curtis Report idea of what a children's officer should be. Her qualification was that she had been secretary to Lady Astor. She possessed an immensely warm heart, a strong sense of humour, and would put down any pomp and ceremony. It showed the climate which still thought of children's officers as those noble women who loved children and got on with people. They did not have to be effective as managers as long as they created a good atmosphere and worked within the budget.

In 1966 I went to East Sussex as children's officer to succeed Joan Cooper who had gone to the Home Office as chief inspector. I received a telegram from former colleagues which stated, "what footsteps to follow." Joan was incredibly helpful in clueing me up about people. I was almost unaware of being a local government employee for all I had wanted to do was to be a social worker in child care. Joan knew how to manage and how to manage councillors and under her direction the children's committee had become a prestigious committee on the county council which was very unusual. It had four former chairmen of the county council on it. They were good and accepted that I was different from Joan. It was not politically divided. When I first went there I could not tell from what members said what party they belonged to. Only later were party groups established. The chair was Rosemary Crawley. Once she understood you and had been allowed freedom to decide for herself, she supported you. She came to staff training courses to learn as well as to teach. She was great. I never declared my own political views but they must have known. It did not matter, they valued the service.

One of the most helpful things that Joan Cooper said to me was that one of the first things to focus on was training. I was already predisposed to that but it was good practical advice because the committee was ready to think of child care officers as professionals and to spend money to that end. I instituted a training scheme in which we took people for a year and then seconded them. It made a more secure base for getting trained people than just relying on those who became available. I set targets for the numbers of trained officers and we achieved over 90 per cent.

Residential staff was an even more desperate need and much more difficult to tackle for it was not only training that was needed but also substantial changes to the nature of residential work. Also residential care was taking increasing proportions of disturbed children because foster care programmes had developed. Trying to obtain trained residential staff was difficult because there was not a nationally accepted professional training. We drew in a few people from child care courses who wanted residential work but mostly it was those who came into it accidentally. I do not think we solved it — that has not happened even now. We did not get a sufficiently equipped body of professional people.

Trying to change institutions from outside was very difficult. I knew what it was like inside for I had worked in an approved school. In East Sussex, I had two approved schools. One was a newly established school which had been set up by Joan Cooper. The other was a good run-of-the-mill school but I considered it was damaging a lot of the kids. With my colleagues in the department, we decided to put resources into changing it. We got in on the selection of staff, which had previously rested with the headmaster. We introduced training programmes for the school staff. But it did not have much impact. The school was subsequently closed in the days of the SSD.

The other school was run by Arthur Laycock who was an artist — appointed by Joan Cooper. He was very much a teacher but he had originality about him. It turned out not a bad place but fairly expensive — probably pioneering up a wrong track. When we were developing it we found ourselves so controlled by the Home Office regulations for approved schools that we needed to break out of them. We did much lobbying and eventually got agreement to the Home Office setting up a Development Group, which included myself and Arthur Laycock and Home Office representatives, to work out afresh what size units to have, what staffing ratios were required, what standards of training. It was published as *Care and Treatment in a Planned Environment*. I did not stay long enough to see what happened following the 1969 Act but changes to our school did get off the ground. Local people were worried both about the costs of changes and having delinquent children near them. But we had fruitful discussions and found that if you were open and the school was open — and Arthur was good at that — they were well disposed to being helpful.

East Sussex had one or two posts called intensive caseworkers who specialized in prevention. But prevention really took the shape of all child care officers knowing what resources were available in order to undertake experimental services. We also encouraged other organizations like the Diocesan Association for Moral Welfare to get interested in Intermediate Treatment. I had been to Northorpe Hall in Yorkshire to look at their approach and came back and talked about that. The Association established a centre in mid-Sussex, took kids and worked closely with us. It was a good model and the department developed other centres. The strategy did prevent children coming into care. It was not just the Children's Department. We tried to influence other departments, including housing. We set up a housing committee: we had to work with eight district councils who had responsibility for homelessness — which was mad: the housing managers were a great strength. Again, we set up a working party between Housing Departments and the Children's Department and produced a report *The Responsibility for Housing the Community* which went to all county and district councillors. This was one of the most successful things we did and it was preventative work because we had almost been driven to receive children into care when they were homeless. I remember having the NSPCC on my back because I said of some children, "It is only a home they want, they do not need care." They replied, "They are sleeping in a car up on the heath." I said, "So be it, let them sleep in a car." We took a strong line on that. Fortunately, we had the support of the committee.

The Association of Children's Officers was a great help and pleasure to me. I became its president. It put me in touch with other children's officers. There were what I called the Curtis Committee children's officers; Gwyneth Wansborough-Jones in Essex, a very competent woman and a good manager; Beryl Watson of Surrey, a barrister; Frances Drake; Lucy Faithful; Mr Holmes in Birmingham whose early report *The First Four Years* was very influential; another man was Colonel Craig of Liverpool who must have gone straight from the army in 1948 — my wife and I were running a youth camp in the Wirral. Craig had rescued a boy from a mental hospital and placed him in a special school and wanted somewhere for him in the holidays. Craig, the children's officer himself, came to see us, we took the boy and he prospered. Craig did not have the right kind of professional background but he would take endless trouble for individual children.

Looking back, I realize that you need to have time, people and continuity to provide care services for children and those who look after them. We came a long way and many Children's Departments did provide these and certainly did appreciate their importance. Anyone who attended the child care courses at LSE could not fail to know how important continuity was to children. The Life Story Books were an acknowledgement of a child's past, present and future. Good Children's Departments demonstrated these values. And the support came. Foster parent groups got going in some areas.

One of the striking things in the 1948 Children Act was that it focused on children and their needs and the child care staff were responsible for meeting them. It meant there was no cross-border bargaining. I was made to understand the importance of this once SSDs were established and I met former chief welfare officers, now in SSDs, who boasted of the battles they had won to avoid financial responsibility for those in need of welfare, the mentally ill, the elderly etc. They had constant cross-border arguments with other departments because there was no definite legislation laid upon them and they had to go to the ministry for arbitration. The Children Act eliminated that for children and had strong implications for the quality of care and the sense of responsibility towards children. There was also the intimacy of child care, you could pick up the phone to any part of the country and know that the person answering would be speaking your language and often you knew that person.

I was in favour of the Seebohm changes. I had worked in the LCC and, as a child care officer, I had received a phone call from a doctor saying, "Mrs X is to be discharged next week. There are three children at home and she won't be in any condition to look after them. You have got to move them". I resisted it. It showed a failure to treat families as a whole. The doctor looked at the patient in such a narrow way as to think that the children were of no importance to the mother. That was a pretty prevalent view and it was a good reason for the Seebohm exercise. Although I had very happy experiences with the East Sussex Children's Department and with the resources and support we got, I knew other departments which were lacking in both.

I became director of East Sussex SSD and stayed until 1981. Sadly, the reforms did not work out. I do not think it is because we were all Seebohm-ized that explains the present disarray. It is the fact that the management of the services is now virtually in the hands of accountants and statisticians. The commitment, the concern for individuals exists in the field workers and the residential care workers but not at the top. So policy decisions are political decisions, the buying and selling of services has intervened. I do not think you can blame Seebohm for that. It is rather the way in which politicians and careerist managers have wanted to control events. The idea of saying that the most important element of a service are the people who receive it — that would not be accepted by managers today.

My approach as a children's officer was to get good staff, help them with training, give them good conditions, and turn them loose to do their best. That gained such a positive response and commitment that it kept them going through all kinds of difficulties and traumas — far longer than the threats of disciplinary action today. Management has been taken over by people who are not primarily interested in the people they are serving. And no amount of restructuring is going to alter that. And this has happened in the voluntary sector as well with the agencies becoming both bigger and also dependent upon statutory bodies for money.

Joan Beckett

Introduction
Joan Beckett was born in Liverpool in 1919. Her family were ship-owners whose fortunes declined during the economic depression. She attended a prep school then Belvedere, a girl's public school, followed by Girton College, Cambridge. After the war, she went to Germany to do relief work which confirmed her interest in social work. Back in Britain, Joan joined the civil service in an administrative capacity but, bored with this, she trained at the LSE as a child care officer before joining the LCC Children's Department. She was children's officer of the London borough of Kensington and Chelsea from 1965-1971 and its deputy director in the Social Services Department from 1971 until her retirement.

Interview
I left Cambridge, people said I was mad, and went to LSE where I was well Winnicotted by Donald and Clare. Clare Winnicott was remarkable, very pretty and intelligent, she became the kind of emblem of what we wanted to be.

Following the LSE., I joined the Children's Department of the London County Council. Donald Winnicott used to say that they trained us to do child care while the LCC mowed us down. It was the hardest work I ever did and I am proud of it. I covered the Westminster-Paddington area. Starting with a caseload of 59 and l hardly ever had a full nights sleep. There was no one to do night duty so you were rung up all through the night and you had to go. The next morning you started at the usual time and just carried on. We were bashed and you had to be tough to take it. I was glad to be there because Cambridge had been too privileged. The trouble was that you always felt guilty about what you were not doing. You had the training to tell you what to do and yet you knew you were not doing it. Fortunately I was pretty healthy and active and got on with it and only had three days sick leave in 30 years. I don't mean that some mornings I didn't get up and feel, "Oh, l don't want to go to work, I've got a bad cold." You just did it. My colleagues, the other child care officers were pretty good and supportive. The area contained rich parts in which lived the wives of professional men. A number of these had trained in child care. They were privileged, their husbands were rich but that did not stop them from being good child care officers. Also, they lived near and so were on the spot.

Eventually I was promoted. I had a row about it because I did not want to move up and I did not want to go to Islington. Fortunately I was soon moved back. During this time, I still had cases and worked with Donald Winnicott in his capacity as a psychiatrist. I would go to his house in Chester Square — what a contrast to the sixty floor council flats I was also visiting — where he only had bananas for lunch. I remember one girl I took regularly and Donald would advise me on the attention I had to give to her. I said "Donald, do you realize all the other things I have to do, like administration?" He replied, "If you were mature, you could decide on your priorities. You've got to concentrate on this girl." But it was a privilege to share in treatment with Donald. And I did stay with that girl right through to the time when she had her own children.

In 1965, when the LCC was abolished, I became children's officer of Kensington and Chelsea. I had been trained in casework and now I had to take over administration. It is sometimes said that social workers are not conscious of costs. Well, I certainly was and had to control the costs of boarding out and children's homes. It also meant that I had to take on a different role when saying 'no' to field work staff who always wanted more resources. The staff in the long-established departments, the Town Hall people, regarded us as rather curious people. They liked us but felt we were an alien culture, a bit odd. They knew that sometimes I would go out at night to deal with some ghastly case and that I provoked a major row rather than take more children into the nursery without more staff! We were social workers not Town Hall officials.

Fortunately, we did have a very good children's committee. It included Bea Serota and Peggy Jay and others of very high calibre. The committee led us and we pushed them. We never had sufficient resources — child care was expensive, particularly as we had a high number of maladjusted children — but the committee did understand what we were doing.

We were criticized by the Home Office inspectors for not having enough foster homes. The trouble was that they were very difficult to find in over-crowded central London and the ones we inherited from the LCC tended to be out in the country. Gradually we did increase the number but never sufficiently. However, the ones we did have did tend to be stable with some of the foster parents showing remarkable staying power. I should mention that abuse is not new and I realized that sometimes physical or sexual abuse did occur in foster homes as well as with natural parents. I also realized that removing the children is not always the answer and indeed can sometimes do more harm. Fortunately, we had no major scandals. In one case, I sent a child care officer to investigate a report; she found no child in the building; I then sent a senior who found a neglected baby in a back room; if she had not done so there could have been a disaster.

We did take over some good children's homes. Above all we had trained child care officers. They were over-worked, had insufficient clerical help and had to write up reports by hand, and went to the limits. They worked so hard at prevention until they could do no more. I was also fortunate in having David Stapleton as my deputy and then Jim Harding joined as a senior child care officer. I was very impressed with Jim, he wrote things up so well.

Despite all the administration, I was determined still to see some individual clients. There was one man, an ex-prisoner — and murderer — who stormed into the office complaining that I would not allow his daughter, who was in care, to go and live with him. I was out but on my return — and against the advice of my staff — I said I would visit him that evening. It was a basement flat and full of bottles of booze. He asked what I wanted to drink and I said tea. We had a bit of a blarney because I would not give way about his daughter. I must have got through. It was the night of the Notting Hill riots and at the end he insisted on escorting me back to the office.

When reorganization was mooted I was in favour because it does make sense to have the whole family dealt with by one department. However, it all went through far too quickly. I did not want to become a director and took on the post of deputy director of social services in Kensington and Chelsea until my retirement. But things are not easy now. I think it is that Children's Departments did a whole lot of real caring and that does not seem to happen now. We made lasting relationships. I still see some of the youngsters who were in our care. Just last week I was thrilled to get a visit from a former child. She was absolutely mature, had a good job, a child. Yet I remember when everyone said she was impossible and could not be fostered. I put her in a middle class foster home and, against all the odds, it lasted.

Joan Cooper

Introduction
Joan Cooper was born in 1914. After graduating from Manchester University, she worked as a housemother at Styal Children's Home. After some teaching and probation work, she was appointed in 1948 as an administrative assistant to the Derbyshire Education Department in order to supervise evacuees which included helping to set up a child guidance clinic. From 1948-1965, Joan Cooper was children's officer of East Sussex. In 1965, she became chief inspector at the Home Office Children's Department and then Director of the Social Work Service at the DHSS. Since retirement she has been an Honorary Visiting Research Fellow at the University of Sussex.

Interview
I started on 5 July, 1948, the day the Children Act came into being. I was thirty-four years old, very young. At the very top of County Hall was a large room which housed two boarding out officers and a clerk. I joined them. I didn't know what to do. There was a copy of the 1948 Children Act placed before me and there were these people who didn't seem to want anything to do with me. It was an uncomfortable first week.

At this stage, the Children's Committee were not entirely sympathetic to the new arrangements. They could not understand the pressure from the Home Office to have a woman because there were not women chief officers in those days. In County Hall, where the committee meetings were held, there was just a men's lavatory for chief officers — I could not go until some of the women committee members said use theirs. Some members were personally supportive of me but in some ways quite resentful of the new fangled ideas and the new expenditures. There was a bit of trouble in the early stages because one council member wanted children to be sent to New Zealand and Australia with their "wonderful opportunities in farming." Fortunately, our chairman invited him and me to lunch and we had it out and he subsided — but not totally.

The children's committee changed from this but it took six to seven years. Then it became the most popular committee and even surpassed education. I can remember a conference between members and staff of the education committee and children's committee because the former was persuaded that we were producing large numbers of very difficult children who were making demands on the education system. The University of Sussex was just starting and the first Vice Chancellor, John Fulton came to the meeting and he and I had a conversation and from that day until this I have had a connection with the university. It gave us a bit of class to have this connection which appealed to the Education Department.

It dawned upon me that we had to make some sort of relationship with welfare services because many of the children were in Part III Accommodation in the depths of the country. Gradually we separated off the children from elderly and handicapped persons. There were large institutions in the middle of Sussex with no transport to reach them. Initially, some of the committee members couldn't see why this should change. This was where casework was introduced to the committee because some of the case studies of these children had a poignancy that they could respond to. There was an enormous institution with over a hundred children, shared by East and West Sussex but run by East Sussex. Apart from the sea of faces, the thing that struck me so much was that families were not encouraged to visit and when they did there was nowhere for them to put their outdoor clothes or to speak to their children in private. These were, in effect, orphans being created by a system. Obviously this large institution had to be got rid of, there was no way you could humanize it. So that was our task.

Then there was an isolated nursery that had the typical institutional look — visitors were not encouraged. I have a memory of children banging their heads all the time against their cot sides. Somehow, for as long as we kept them, these institutions had to be humanized and run in the interests of children and families rather than staff.

The rage of the time was for small children's homes of about 9-12 children. This took a good deal of selling to the committee because they thought it would inevitably be more expensive. It wasn't in fact because the big homes meant a host of cleaning and supervisory staff and the smaller homes were more economical. But we underestimated the problems of small homes, the demands made on staff who got so little time off, and it was difficult to recruit assistant staff. But the children were clearly much more at home. I remember some children from a small home going on a seaside holiday and when they returned they literally ran from the bus, up the stairs and flung themselves on their own individual beds. It really was quite heartening to see the show of emotion and pleasure at their way of life. So for a time I became enamoured with small homes and it was much easier to arrange for the families to visit.

The nightmare was to recruit residential staff. We had inherited an approved school from the LCC, a huge institution. Then the Home Office persuaded us to start from scratch another one which was not to be in the depths of the country but the disaster was again staffing. Where did you get them? Either they came from traditional approved schools and were ill-at-ease in a new kind of situation or you could not get them at all. I was very interested in delinquency but I felt that this part of our work was pretty much a failure. We were asked to start a girls' remand home for all of south-east England — the staffing was impossible and we were having to spare child care officers to stand-in. I myself stood in quite a lot. We could not easily get staff of any kind and to get educated staff — which was necessary for these extremely disturbed girls — proved impossible.

Then there was fostering. The big problem was that the LCC had its own staff operating in Sussex to board out London children. We felt very resentful about this and complained bitterly to the Home Office and the LCC. The LCC could not see that it was possible to find foster homes in London and, in any case, considered that it was healthier to put children in the country — health was a big concern then. In time we resolved it. I got appointed to the Home Office Advisory Council in Child Care and it became a forum in which to complain and to explain. There was some support from other areas for the LCC also had staff stretching from Suffolk to Sussex and the LCC began to see the possibility of finding foster homes within its own area. I am bound to say that we also followed this practice and looked for foster homes in the rural areas, partly because in the towns there was work for women. But it also made for difficulties because the country was inaccessible and much harder for families to keep in touch. The boarding out officers did have cars. I appointed one officer who couldn't even drive and she now informs me that I told her firmly to take driving lessons and to appear within a month with a car.

A section of work which was heavy in East Sussex was private homes and schools which had to be inspected. This caused some resentment from the committee and staff. And some were difficult places with some of their children having to come before the juvenile court. It could also be difficult for our officers going to well-known schools where their staff gave them short-shrift.

I was very keen that we should create a reputation for having trained staff. I think we only had two untrained child care officers while I was there. The staff numbers expanded rapidly. They had to. If you were going to create a system of small children's homes instead of large institutions, there was an enormous amount of work to do. Some of the children had to be rehabilitated at home; some went to small homes; in each case a really good case history had to be built up and this took the time of trained staff who knew what they were looking for.

The committee, after five to six years, got gripped by the work. They were behind our emphasis on training. Also they were very generous in letting me travel abroad. I went to Holland to study their methods of dealing with physically and mentally handicapped children which were well in advance of ours. I came back and said we must have different standards and ambitions for these children because if it can be achieved in Holland it can be achieved here. Then we got someone from Holland to reinforce that. I went to America on a scholarship and came back full of group work and, after one committee meeting was over, gave the children's committee a lecture on it. I said that if we were to develop group work then we were going to have to have in each of our area offices a group work room in order that we could get in people from the locality and introduce group work to them. There was a very tense debate about this — "the children's officer always wants to spend money". I left things and spoke again at the next meeting and had some success.

I also went to Texas where I did some lecturing. This was a great opportunity and, as I liked travelling, it was a delight for me. The contacts I made later bore fruit in the Home Office. France, at that time, employed psychologists rather than social workers for fostering children. That was an interesting thought and reinforced a growing relationship with the child guidance clinic and psychiatry.

We had a new psychiatrist at one stage who got very fascinated with children's work and the county medical officer said. "Is he on your staff or mine? I think you had better pay for him." So we had to sort that out. We had always used the clinic and then we began to have meetings with a representative from the Education Department, the Architect Department, the Children's Department and others to try to plan developments. These meetings came to the ears of some of the committee who asked, "Are you usurping our responsibilities?" We replied, "No, we were just formulating ideas. You must have some co-ordinating if ideas are to be produced". And this was accepted.

The committee was also very generous in acknowledging that I needed time off for some public work and I became president of the Association of Children's Officers in 1954. Committee members also came to the conferences and lectures and I felt supported. There was an interesting incident at the end of the association's annual dinner when the guest of honour was Arthur Miller, father of Jonathan. He said to me "Joan, you have something to say but you say it very badly. Now you must go and get some elocution lessons and if you can't afford it, I'll find a medical charity." I found a local drama school, managed to afford the lessons, and it proved very good advice and I've always been grateful.

I think that given the history and geography of East Sussex and the quality of committee membership, we were able to develop a pretty sophisticated service. We were not deeply involved in poverty. I don't know what social workers can do about it. Poverty is a determining factor in the lives of children but social workers can not cure it. There is rural poverty but that is hidden, and was little recognized at that time. Rural poverty, like any poverty was real enough — if you are hungry, you are hungry. But that was not our main function which was to recognize talent and to help individual children to develop it and to maintain links with their families.

We encouraged the education of our children, we wanted them to stay on at school and, when I left, we had six children at university. That does not sound very many but Kellmer Pringle did a comparative study with Birmingham and found that it had only two amongst a much higher population. If East Sussex Children's Department had strength it was in sophistication rather than in tackling poverty.

Children's Departments were intimate in a way that SSDs, because of size, can no longer be. Attention was focused on children and didn't have the rivalry of the elderly, mentally ill and so on. But it had the faults of too small size in some cases; its professionalism was sometimes sacrificed to the demands of Children's Departments who would evolve on the casework side and I hoped they would develop group work and community work. Community work got lost in the Home Office and, although a number of papers were written about it, it never took off.

There was an enormous variation in standards up and down the country and, although we had a large inspectorate charged with the duty of equalizing standards, this was not easy because local government is designed to be local but to have national standards. My personal ambition was to try and humanize the approved schools but we did not succeed. There was too much history behind, and too much tradition in the Home Office dealing with people in large number — prisons, for instance. If you look at the evidence the Home Office gave to the Seebohm Committee, one of their arguments was that the Home Office needed the Children's Departments as it had to have something which is seen by the general public to be forward looking and humane — unlike prisons and the restriction of liberty. It was a poor argument.

I was deeply involved in the Children and Young Persons Act (1969) and if I was to try and defend myself I would say that my energies went into legislation to do something about the approved schools. Approved schools disliked it, abused it, they were antagonistic. I had to spend a lot of time meeting their association's committee. But they clung to their traditions and the military model because it was what they knew.

Compared with what I saw in 1948, with those old, large institutions, the Children's Departments did bring about great improvements. The finding of foster homes improved and we got away from the "we can't do it in this town" attitude. The departments did produce some outstanding children's officers such as Sylvia Watson, Elizabeth Harvie, Brian Roycroft, Barbara Kahan and Bill Craig. The women children's officers were, on the whole, better educated than the men and they felt they had to do a special job, otherwise they would have been letting their colleagues down, letting the service down, they would for ever have sealed the doom of women as chief officers in local government. I don't mean this is conscious but I think there was some sort of culture like this. We had a sense of mission but today, how can you have a sense of mission about constantly assessing people for services? — I would find that difficult.

Children's Departments did play a part in the development of the social work profession but not as an important a part as medical social workers and psychiatric social workers, who were much more consciously social workers. Many Children's Departments' people thought that child care officers were a different and distinct profession and that is a sadness to be regretted.

It is very difficult to say whether the Seebohm changes were a success. The trouble is that it is hard to say how it would have developed if the managerial revolution had not happened. I am bothered that we have a lawyer as chair of CCETSW. Why do we have to go to a different profession? We have not been able to produce a director of CCETSW who is a qualified social worker. I feel there is something wrong with the training of social workers. They seem to have taken on — or agreed to have imposed upon them — this assessment process which was developed by Griffiths, who had no previous knowledge of the social services. So I do not feel that the profession has yet established itself in its own opinion or in the world's opinion. Of course, it must be said that the government is not encouraging any profession to be creative.

I would like to see social work much more confident, more restricted in what it will undertake. If you look at the columns in *Community Care* in which social workers seek help on a subject, the variety is fantastic. Unless you have training the length of doctors and lawyers, it is not possible. In another sense I think social work is under ambitious. It doesn't claim kudos when it should, as for example in fostering which is an important contribution to social work. I am sad that community work has not developed to any extent because this is a cementing situation with localities which could help meet some of the problems of an ageing population and a population in which people with handicaps survive longer — and I do not see how you can for ever do this on an individual basis. And this community work should be by SSD's because they can pick up the problems and use resources appropriately. If there was more community development, there would be fewer child abuse cases.

Frances Drake

Introduction

Frances Drake was born in 1920 and went to school in Bradford. She took a degree in English at Cambridge University before attending the London School of Economics. From 1944-1948 she worked as an HM Inspector of Factories. From 1948-1970 she was the children's officer for Northamptonshire. She then served as that county's director of social services until her retirement in 1974.

Interview

Like most of the first children's officers, I was motivated to take up the work by the descriptions in the Curtis Report of the conditions of children in care. When I was appointed, aged 28, I was the youngest children's officer. I subsequently realized that one reason they took me was that some felt I was so young and inexperienced I could be easily manipulated. Both the chief welfare officer and the medical officer of health wanted control over the children's services. Initially, I was responsible to the welfare officer who tried to sign all my letters but, as I told him, he could not sign as children's officer and this argument and many other similar petty power struggles gradually petered out.

When I took up my appointment, the staff consisted of one boarding-out officer, half the time of one clerk, and a part-time typist. People from other departments staggered in to dump stacks of files on my floor. The clerk elected to do over-time and we sat for hours sorting out the files of children who had been divided between welfare, health and education. It resulted in a new co-ordinated system and set of forms. Reading the files also showed me that foster children had often been visited by elected members who did not write reports but who ticked a few boxes on a form. I realized we needed more information.

I was allowed to attend a meeting of the welfare committee so that I could see what happened at committees. At the next children's committee in three months time, I would have to give a report on how we should implement the 1948 Children Act. I drew up a plan for dividing the county into areas with a child care officer to be responsible in each, and setting out what they should be doing. It was agreed that I should have five child care officers, two typists, the clerk to be full-time and a junior clerk I was also granted a deputy.

The geographical arrangements of my department were peculiar. I had a tiny office still with the blackout curtains, my deputy had a similar one some distance away near the ladies' lavatories but with no telephone. To get in touch with her, I had to send a runner. The rest of the staff were upstairs in the Welfare Department's general office.

My chairman was a very intelligent woman, widely known and involved in very many committees. At first, she was rather cautious in her approach to me, fearing that her reputation might by ruined by the activities of this child. Over the years, she gave me her full support and was a person for whom I still retain the greatest admiration and affection.

We took over a mixture of children's homes. A small home for eight difficult boys, about 20 miles away, was highly unpopular in the village as the boys did things like spitting in the milk churns. The vicar would not have them in the church unless both the superintendent and the matron accompanied them. Another home had 30 children and was run extremely rigidly by a superintendent and matron who regarded the children as personal servants, useful for bringing them cups of tea in bed. The couple were highly popular with local notables because they kept such tight control over the children. Another large home was split into two houses also under unsuitable staff. Much better was a hostel in Kettering which had been for unbilletable evacuees. It had a delightful matron who always managed to accept and love each individual child, however unappealing.

We had no provision of our own for babies but were allowed to use two small residential nurseries run by the Welfare Department for their own families. I remember standing in telephone boxes, late at night with rain dripping off me, and asking the matrons to take a baby. We were frequently told they had no beds and we had to take the babies home ourselves. I unkindly hoped that when one of the matrons was knocking at heaven's door she would be told they had no beds.

Later we took over a residential nursery from the Health Department which relieved the situation. This was originally for short-stay children and had no stock of clothes or bedding. It seemed to keep going on blankets and eiderdowns sent during the war from the U. S. A.

Our first task was to improve the homes. The chairman went to one of the small nurseries and found some sub-normal children tied to their chairs, shades of the Curtis Report. The superintendent, who was so rigid, hit a child on the head with a stick and we were able to get rid of him and his wife. The couple in the large home fell foul of the auditors by having strawberries for themselves billed as cabbages and clothing. Decorating and re-furnishing took place slowly and we opened small homes and a second nursery. I hoped to have a range of homes of different kinds.

Later I changed the functions of the nurseries and matrons. A small unit for six very difficult and medically unfit babies was opened in a family home. A group of foster homes was set up to take the number of babies and toddlers who would have previously gone into the larger nursery. This became an "extra mural" nursery and the matron who ran the unit for the six very ill or ill-treated babies was also responsible for visiting the foster mothers. She had been used to a nursery where every kind of hygienic provision had been made. The medical officer of health asked how often the lavatory chains were cleaned. In the foster families she visited, she saw them licking dummies and sticking them in sugar. She came back horrified and I said to her, "That's life". The children were no more likely to be ill than in the nursery. She got used to it. She knew about babies and if she thought anything was wrong, she got in touch with the child care officer and they would visit together and if necessary the baby was admitted to the small unit.

Another nurse was appointed to visit all the other babies who were fostered but were not part of the extra-mural unit. She also visited babies and children in their own homes if there was a suspicion of neglect or ill-treatment. She was closely in touch with the health visitors and the paediatricians in one of the local hospitals. This was in addition to the statutory visits made by the child care officers.

Because, over the years, the committee was very supportive, I was able to introduce a number of progressive ideas. One home dealt with maladjusted children with severe behavioural problems. I thought it wrong that such homes should be isolated in the country so I planned to have a strong community link. During the day, treatment and teaching were provided in the main building with a tolerant regime. Classes were no more than five children. No corporal punishment and discipline to depend on the relationship formed by the teacher. An educational psychologist was in charge and he arranged regular visits from the child psychiatrist, mainly to support the staff. At night the children returned to three family group homes where they were expected to behave normally. It worked very well. The head never refused a child or asked for one to be removed. One member of staff was engaged in working with the families of the children and working out future plans and placements. We tried a number of other unusual regimes.

Initially, the child care officers were predominantly graduates with some social work experience. Eventually, we refused to appoint any who were not professionally qualified. Most of us had been through the war and were used to acting independently. People were also used to taking orders. We discussed what was wanted, how to do it, then got on with it. There was a very good spirit. The need "to clarify the role" came very much later. Considerable energy was devoted to fostering and the numbers fostered rose proportionately. There was a lot of co-operation with probation officers, the NSPCC, educational welfare officers and health visitors at a very personal level. Life in a local authority was much less formal and "chummier" than the civil service which I had been used to. The child care officers became familiar figures in the courts, presenting reports and conveying juvenile delinquents to approved schools.

We were not aware of the amount of sexual abuse that seems to take place today. The existence in isolated villages of incest was known but we were mainly concerned with neglect and physical abuse. I was a member of the Tunbridge Well's Study Group which was concerned with studying the problem parents who were said to "batter" their children. After the Children and Young Persons Act (1963) we developed preventative work so that by the final year we had 255 families under rehabilitative supervision and a specially designed hostel for difficult problem families. Play groups were set up in a number of children's homes to be used by neighbouring families. It was not just the child care officers and residential staff. We made arrangements for the clerical workers to visit the homes as well.

Throughout all this, we increasingly recognized the value of relationships and the harm which could be done every time a child was moved. We realized that a new children's home was of little use if the relationships within it were poor.

I was the last president of the Association of Children's Officers and would like to quote something from my presidential address in 1970 because it says in brief what I have been saying now:

> Those of us who were fortunate enough to come into the child care field in 1948 were committed to the idea of change — our terms of reference were clear, we had a number of obvious defects to remedy, an inspiring task to perform and we wanted to use our energies to make things better as we saw them. I think we should be lacking in proper feelings were we not to take some pride in saying that what we were then called upon to do we have done and very much more.

I had mixed feelings about the Seebohm proposals. Everyone wanted the social services to become more important. A director would have more clout than a children's officer and it was important that social workers got into these positions. What was not recognized was the problems of putting together departments with very different standards of work but with expectations of improvement. Increasing legislation without comparable funding has meant that the quality of work of some child care workers has deteriorated. In the past a children officer was a known figure to staff and children. A director is too often a person totally aloof.

Bill Freeman

Introduction

Bill Freeman was born in 1914 in Liverpool. His mother died when he was three and he was brought up by grandparents and aunts. He went to school and university in Liverpool where he did a degree in social science. Bill saw the enormous poverty and the system of casual employment in Liverpool. In 1937, he became a Home Office trainee in the probation service and was resident at Toynbee Hall in London. From 1938-40, he worked as a probation officer in Birmingham before joining the army where he was commissioned. After the war he returned to the probation service in Liverpool. He was children's officer for Warrington 1948-51, for Bolton 1951-55, and

Sheffield 1955-1970. After reorganization of the personal social services, he was director of social services Leeds 1970-74 and then for Leeds Metropolitan District 1974 until his retirement in 1978.

Interview

On my first morning as children's officer at Warrington, the town clerk didn't know who I was. I don't think they wanted a new department. They knew nothing about social work and I think they wanted the medical officer of health to take over. There was no office for me. Nowhere even to sit. All I had was the 1948 Children's Act, the Curtis Report and my own experience in probation plus five years voluntary social work in Liverpool. At first I was the only person in the Children's Department. Somebody said to me, "You've got Padgate Cottage Homes, you know." I asked how many children were there and was told 200, although 100 belonged to the county. I went out and found a large place, buzzing with life. Warrington also had children in voluntary homes, some in the south of England. Almost immediately I heard we had a girl boarded out by the Education Department in a foster home in St Helen's which was breaking down. I went and fetched her. Then I was handed 160 case papers. I was given an office with the Registrar for Births and Deaths and later lent a secretary for two days a week and that was my department.

I found out that the Education Department had been looking after some children under fit person orders while the Health Department had others. These now passed to the Children's Department. I went to the Health Department and met the deputy medical officer of health. He was an old friend of mine from Liverpool University. Then I bumped into the deputy town clerk who also came from Liverpool, as did the chief welfare officer. We became good friends and co-operated well. The chairman of the children's committee was a railway man and the vice chair a butcher. I did not know anything about committee work and so the chief welfare officer took the first committee meeting and I learnt a great deal. Committee members were very important. They lived amongst the people they represented. They visited children's homes, they knew many of the foster children. They knew at first hand what was going on. They were a great help, the chairman in particular. They were often our eyes and ears. I got very excited about local government, all sorts of things were happening. I had to tell the committee what we could and could not do according to the law. I learnt that you had to consult members from other departments. I also had meetings with the chief constable. To me, it was full of excitement.

I had to find some full-time staff and the only person I could find was Margaret Howgate, a probation officer and she was a great asset. We put an advert in the local press for foster parents and got 40 replies. So the two of us had to get round to the 40, supervise fosterings, look after child protection and the cottage homes. I found we had two children sent by the Poor Law to the south of England and I went to sort that out. We did it but it meant working around the clock.

I needed to meet other children's officers. I did so and I valued their special knowledge, especially Ian Brown of Manchester who was first rate. Then just as I was settling, I was in my office one day when I got a phone call from the borough engineer to say that the Home Office inspectorate were here. They informed me that I had to produce a development report within 11 days. I used the Curtis Report to set out the lines of the report, close the cottage homes, start a reception centre, board-out as many children as possible, set up family group homes and get people trained. I had trouble straight away because people liked the cottage homes. The committee were good and started to back me. I took the chair and deputy to Bradford where Arthur Gomersall had started family group homes. My chairman was also mayor of Warrington and the lord mayor of Bradford gave us a marvellous reception and then we saw the well-run homes. The committee agreed to the development report and then we proceeded with family group homes by joining together two semi-detached council houses to take four children. Gradually we ran down the cottage homes.

It was hard work. One Christmas Eve I got a telephone message to say that the boiler had broken down in the boys' hostel so I had to run about to get a new one. I was involved with the committee, voluntary agencies, the churches and, of course, the children. I knew practically every child in care. I remember one sports' day at the cottage homes: one girl was marvellous — she was about 14, lovely golden hair — and she won the cup. When we presented it she looked at the inscription and burst into tears: it still said 'Board of Guardians'. It was terrible. Shades of the Poor Law!

I loved Warrington but the salary scale was £395-435 and I had to provide a car. I had a home, wife, and two children to educate. Bolton was offering a bit more so I went there. I built up a marvellous team: Ann Riley, a social worker, Doris Houghton, a former health visitor, and Margaret Turner, a former teacher, all with child care training. We had to close the cottage homes, set up a reception centre and board out more children. The great thing was that we were in the same building as the Health Department. If we were bothered about a family we could nip along the corridor to consult the assistant medical officer and sometimes did joint visits with health visitors. The co-operation was good.

Then I had my famous Myerscough family. I had become very interested in preventative work and rehabilitation. The NSPCC were going mad about this family, the home conditions were appalling, the Housing Department was complaining, the children were often away from school — the father, when in work, was a long-distance lorry driver and often took the kids with him! One morning the NSPCC brought the children in, the youngest was nine months and the eldest was 15. He said he was going to charge the parents with neglect. I had not got enough places so I rang up Warrington because the closure of their cottage homes had still not been completed and they agreed to keep all the family together. After six months the mother came out of prison and said she wanted them back. I persuaded the Housing Department to give them another house. The Family Service Unit helped them set up house and obtained some furniture. Then the rent collector told the mother off because she was £4 in arrears and she hit him with a stick. I persuaded them not to prosecute. I went round one Christmas and they had no food and I had to supply some. They settled down and, when I left Bolton after five years, I went to see the mother: the father was working, some of the children were in work, there was a strong bond between them. The mother had ten children, six miscarriages, diabetes, a husband in casual work, how could she manage? And ten years later they were still going strong. I wrote this up and showed that it was pointless keeping children in care if the parents, with help, could look after them properly.

In Bolton we closed the cottage homes and set up family group homes. We built a modern residential nursery which was out of date the day we opened it. The Home Office inspector said, "We've changed our minds. We no longer want the tiny children split off from other children. We want them in family groups".

Bolton, with a population of 188,000, was an ideal size. I knew every child. The residential staff were not as well trained as the field staff where we had a good team, all trained, well-balanced. But, in the end, my big chance came, when I was appointed to Sheffield which had a population of 500, 000.

Sheffield was in turmoil. The previous children's officer had to resign. I was offered the job after the committee deliberated for two hours. I don't think the chairman really wanted me. Then I built up my staff: Mary Armitage as deputy, she came from medical social work and knew little about child care and local government but she learnt quickly and was first rate: young Neil Kay came from Cambridge: and Rachel Jenkins and many others.

Dame Grace Tebbitt became chair of the children's committee and was very supportive. The town clerk and the medical officer gave their backing. Again, we closed the cottage homes and turned that into a girl's approved school called Moorside. We were prepared to experiment and sent some girl's out to work. We had one girl, very clever, she had been expelled from three public schools, she threatened suicide, wrote poems about death, created havoc. In the end she became a reporter with a national paper. We had three social workers based at the approved school as well as teachers and house staff. We opened family group homes. We reduced the size of residential nurseries because of the dangers of cross-infection.

We developed fostering. The boarding-out allowances paid by Sheffield were too low. Rachel Jenkins did a study and showed that foster parents did best when properly paid. If paid too little they became too possessive with the children and this caused difficulties. Eventually we pushed the fostering rate up to the very high one of 70 per cent. Rachel, who had led the charge, then said, "We've reached the limit." We had one very difficult case in which the press got involved. The foster mother could cope with very young children but not older ones. In fact, she wanted her own older children taken into care. We decided to remove the small foster child and she went to the press. A national paper published a photo of all the council saying they would decide the child's fate. I could not explain the details to the press but I did to the council and they backed me. If not, I may have had to resign.

Once the untrained staff in one of the family group homes could not cope with the eight boys. I could not find any relief staff for the weekend so I went in myself. I took them for a ramble. We got the bus and there was a row on that straight away which I had to quell. Within half an hour of getting off the bus I had lost them. It was dreadful. I found them and took them to an open air swimming pool: after ten minutes the man in charge said, "Get them away, that kid can't swim and he's going off the top diving board. I won't charge you but just take them away." I got them home for tea then I decided we would play cricket. I said, "Don't hit the ball hard." The first thing they did was to put the ball through a window. Then the tap got turned on in the washroom so we had to mop that up. There was a knock on the door and a policeman stood there and said, "These two kids outside, are they yours?" I saw they were on two bikes which they must have stolen. The policeman said, "Don't you know what's wrong? The brakes don't work on the bikes." I promised to get them seen to. As he went, the policeman said, "You don't know much about this game, do you? Does the boss know?" I replied, "He knows alright." I gave the children supper and put them to bed at 10 o'clock and thought I would have a cup of tea. Then a boy came downstairs and announced, "They've gone, all seven of them." I thought of the headlines the next morning, they had all been in trouble with the police. I was just going to phone the police when there was a knock on the door and they all came back.

The next morning, they would not go to Sunday school so I held a little service. I tried to talk about Daniel in the lion's den. Half-way through the morning, one of the boys said, "They've set fire to the old prefab." So I had to rush round with a fire extinguisher to put it out. In the afternoon I arranged for some to go to Sherwood Forest with the Beetle Motor Club. I had a peaceful afternoon and then at about 4 o'clock a 20 year old girl arrived: she was the new housemother. I rang her up the next morning and she reported that they had quietened down. I would like to pay tribute to our residential house staff, trained and untrained. I wondered about that young girl — then it dawned on me. The boys treated her as a big sister who knew all their tricks. She said, "They knew who you were and they were just showing off." She laughed. It showed me what the residential staff do.

While I was in Sheffield, Barbara Kahan and others went into staffing problems and produced a report of staff-child ratios. The residential staff were the least trained yet were looking after very difficult children. We had set up a classifying centre within the girls' approved school system and did a survey of 100 girls: it established that they were more sinned against than sinning, some had been sexually abused. We needed trained staff in residential establishments and that meant more training courses. The one-year course was not sufficient. We began to run in-service training and set up a student unit with a training officer. Staff selection was also important for some of the candidates were very unsuitable — including paedophiles. Any success I had was due to finding the right staff for the right job. Men and women can be found who can really cope with the children — especially if given some training.

There were weaknesses in the child care service. Caseloads were often too high. Sometimes a lack of supervision over inexperienced officers who had very difficult cases. There were gaps in co-ordination. But the main limitation was what happened to children after eighteen when they left care. There were very few hostels for them, little back-up, we could give little financial help. I'd like to know what happened to the hundreds of children who passed through our care. How did they get on? Of course, many were settled in good foster homes before they reached eighteen years, you never hear of them. I recently heard from a former colleague in Sheffield of a child in care, now married with two children and doing fine. I remember one bright child who could not settle anywhere. His mother was a prostitute. Aged fourteen and at the reception centre, he turned to the warden and said "she doesn't want me, does she?" He came to terms with it. We boarded him out and in the end he went to university. I'd like to know what happened to him. Another boy in care went to Cambridge and, after a good history degree, became a councillor and the chair of a children's committee. These were the stars but what of the others?

The success was that a viable service was created. We improved life for a lot of children. We were both compassionate and pragmatic. You had to have your feet on the ground with these children, we knew they could be like little angels yet also do ridiculous things. We changed our stance from one of seeing ourselves as parents to them, to that of being their trustees. We managed to change people's attitudes towards child care.

Having women children's officers was a tremendous boost. I can't praise them too much. They usually had better degrees than the men, often Oxford and Cambridge graduates. Sylvia Watson, Barbara Kahan, Beti Jones. They had drive and zest. And a woman chief officer was a new thing in local authorities. The Association of Children's Officers was vital. We met regularly, had conferences, shared knowledge and experience. Kenneth Brill was the secretary. We had good speakers for the conferences. When I was president in 1968 we had Lord Seebohm and Lord Kilbrandon plus Joan Cooper, Jean Heywood and Barbara Kahan who were all stars in their own right.

I was all for Seebohm. I had a friend at the Home Office who rang me one Friday in 1968 — when I was president — to say that there was a cabinet meeting on the Monday to make decisions about the Seebohm Report. He said, "Can you get a letter to

Richard Crossman and Jim Callaghan immediately". I did the letters urging the creation of Social Services Departments within local authorities and charged down the Ml on Sunday afternoon and put the letters into the cabinet office. I received replies from both expressing agreement.

After 15 years in Sheffield I was looking forward to applying for the new post as director of the Social Services Department there. I got a hint that I was not the favoured person. I told my chair that Leeds was advertising and she advised me to apply. I was appointed and given a warm welcome. There was an outcry in the press as to why I was leaving. I am glad to say that Mary Armitage, who had left Sheffield some years previously to be children's officer in Cumberland, got the Sheffield job.

At the time I had no doubts about the Seebohm reforms. Now I am not so sure. One of the losses was the Home Office inspectorate. They used to make a proper inspection and it was valuable. They went through procedures and rules and told you how many times you'd broken them. This became advisory just before the social services took over. Incidentally, it was a mistake to remove medical officers of health and health visitors from local authorities. Social Services Departments have become very large and difficult to administer. In Leeds (population 735,000), I had over 2,300 beds for elderly people, mentally and physically handicapped people, over 800 children (including three approved schools), five decentralized divisional offices plus sub-offices, home help service, meals on wheels, a homeless families unit, home teachers for the blind — thousands of staff — and a budget of £21 million. Frankly, it was too large. It was like a gigantic jigsaw puzzle and very hard to put together.

Today I think social work training should be at least three years and a professional register should be set-up. In 1970 at the last meeting of the Association of Social Workers of Great Britain, of which I was treasurer, I advocated the setting up of a professional register of qualified social workers. I lost the motion by one vote. There has been some unfair criticism and bad publicity. The noisy failures give the wrong impression of the service. Some very good work is being done by good people. But I am not sure whether the amalgamation of children's with other services was a good thing. I think children's and welfare services should be separate. The mental health service should be a separate service too; people need a very special training for that. I did not advocate the generic social worker. Child care is highly specialized. The children's officer was responsible for children in care and close supervision was essential. I made sure I was covered, I even wrote regulations like, "you put cold water in the bath first". You went into detail. The children came first and foremost. On balance I would go for a separate service.

Philip Hughes

Introduction

Born in 1922, Philip Hughes moved frequently as his father was a Methodist minister. After attending Kingswood School, he joined the merchant navy as a radio officer. He was on the convoy in which *The City of Benares,* carrying children to evacuation, was torpedoed. Subsequently, Philip Hughes became a pilot in the Fleet Air Arm. Following the war, he studied at Cambridge University and the London School of Economics before working in three residential establishments including the Mulberry Bush School. After further training on the Advanced Casework Course at the Tavistock Clinic, he headed-up the Welfare Services in Cyprus where he and his wife took in and later adopted two local children. From 1959-1965 he was deputy children's officer in Kent and then from 1965-1970 was children's officer in Greenwich. After a short period as children's officer of West Riding, he was appointed director of social services for West Riding and, after local government reorganization, was director for Wakefield Metropolitan District until his retirement in 1985.

Interview

When I started in Kent as deputy children's officer, I was rather taken aback when the assistant clerk, responsible for the Children's Department, took me aside and said that the council was very concerned that so many children were in care and it was looking to me to do something about it. I did find that children were too easily taken into care. I think the Curtis Report made a fundamental mistake when it assumed that children's officers should be women and would be mother figures. I reckon that some of them thought it was almost good to be in care and hence prevention was not quickly developed. None the less, these female children's officers were a most remarkable group of women — Joan Cooper, Sylvia Watson, Beryl Watson, Lucy Faithfull, Barbara Kahan — and they had a great influence on me. The children's officer in Kent was one of them, Elizabeth Harvie, a wonderful person. Her caring for children was shown in the large number who kept in contact with her after they went out of care. These children's officers really did care for children. Today some of the top people in Social Services Departments, which is now big business, may be good administrators but I am not sure that they have the same concern for children and families, the desire to build a better Britain. Their concern is more likely to be to carve out a career. I suppose it was that those women came into being at a time of idealism, at the creation of the welfare state, and it fired them with enthusiasm.

In Kent I was concerned to find a low proportion of qualified staff. We did succeed in taking on more qualified child care officers but had less success with residential staff. And numbers in care did fall steadily for a few years.

After five years came the reorganization of the London County Council (LCC) with Kent shedding large areas to the new boroughs. In 1965 I was appointed children's officer for Greenwich. We had to work at taking on children's homes that had come under the LCC and at sharing facilities with other London boroughs. Fortunately, I had a very good team with Margaret Evans as my deputy. By offering good working conditions, we appointed a high number of qualified child care officers working within area teams. We had only seven or eight small children's homes. I have always considered it important for senior people to keep in close touch with the residential establishments. It makes for better staff relationships and it means you get to know the children. The residential staff were mainly unqualified but they did a good job. We decided to have our own observation centre with John Williams in charge. It was a great success for John had tremendous knowledge of residential child care. We were also developing boarding-out. I recognized that for most children fostering was the best option although there is always a place for high quality residential care.

The children's committee gave us good backing. It was a Labour council who were trying to build a good community. So things were going well. But, at the time, more reorganization was in the air. Some advocated that children's work should come under health. I regarded this as a retrograde step for children's services always suffer by becoming a fringe activity of education or health instead of being the central focus of a department. The Seebohm committee was in session and it was anticipated that it would recommend a new and independent Social Services Department. However, Greenwich had members who did favour a health takeover. It also had a live wire of a medical officer of health who was competent but without real understanding of people. I remember him saying that it did not matter where a new old peoples home was to be located, it could be the North Pole if necessary. Just then the Home Office asked me to apply to be children's officer at the West Riding where the incumbent was about to retire. I got the post.

When I was appointed to West Riding, I remember asking the clerk of the council if I was now a chief officer. He replied, "No, you are the head of a minor department." His statement illustrated the attitude of many clerks towards the Children's Departments. I found few qualified staff and morale pretty low. I put forward a scheme for restructuring the department with more and better paid senior posts. However, we had not got far when the Seebohm reforms came into being and I was appointed director of social services for the West Riding.

I think the creation of Social Services Departments was right. Previously different groups of people were too divided. But the departments need resources. If you are to have high quality casework then social workers must have small caseloads. I know of one authority where they do have under twenty cases each and do a remarkably good job with them. The problem is that some people get no service at all. I was appalled to learn that half the children on the at risk register had not been allocated to a social worker. I think directors now have a terrible job because they don't have sufficient resources. It also worries me to read of so many unnecessary scandals which stem from a lack of co-operation between social workers and health visitors or education officials.

The amalgamation of the children's and other services into one Social Services Department did lead to a stronger department. Directors are chief officers and I think the Association of Directors of Social Services (ADSS) had more clout than the Association of Children's Officers. The ADSS had regular meetings with the Secretary for State for Social Services. I must add that of late the ADSS does not seem to have put up much of a fight against the government's intention of making local authorities act less as providers of services and more into agents who direct, for instance, the elderly into private old people's homes. Much credit must be given to Children's Departments. In a fairly short period of time they professionalized a service which before had been run in health and education settings by untrained people. They set new standards in children's homes. They pushed fostering into prominence as probably the best way of looking after children away from their parents.

Noel Hustler

Introduction
Noel Hustler was born in 1921 and brought up in Ipswich. He won a scholarship to Ipswich School where he refused to join the officers training corps. As his father was unemployed, he turned down the opportunity of going to university and took a job as a junior clerk with the General Accident Insurance Company. In his spare time he worked with refugee children. In 1939 he linked up with the Quakers, joined the Peace Pledge Union, and worked on a pacifist farming community. Towards the end of the war, by then married, he worked in residential hostels. After the war, he became a probation officer for ten years until joining the London County Council (LCC) Children's Department as a senior child care officer in 1959. He transferred to the LCC's Mental Health Department before rejoining its children's service as an inspector in 1962. He was children's officer of Lewisham from 1965-1971. He served as director of the Social Services Department at Bexley until his retirement.

Interview
In 1962 there arose a vacancy at the inspectorate of the LCC's Children's Department and I was appointed. The London County Council was the only Children's Department to have its own inspectorate — six inspectors, including Mr Fitzgerald, who pushed it forward, and Ken Urwin who later became the children's officer at Camden. It was an interesting job with 10,000 children in care, but difficulties existed in that the inspectorate had no executive function, it was just to advise. The power tended to be with administrative officers, none of whom were social workers. The LCC was too vast, it was an administrative machine, I hardly ever met a member of its children's committee. It had five large children's homes scattered throughout London, each with 400-500 children, all with their own laundries, swimming pools and all very institutionalized. There was a vast Supplies Department with all the clothes, swimming

45

costumes, towels, marked "LCC". The children's officer was Wilson Wheeler but I never met him. He departed suddenly in 1962 and rather than advertise, the LCC added the duties to that of the existing deputy clerk to the council.

The LCC was dissolved in 1965 and replaced by twelve local authorities. I was made children's officer for Lewisham with Robin Osmond as one of the senior child care officers. The twelve Children's Departments varied greatly. Some still retained one of the enormous children's homes. In Lewisham, the members of the council displayed both ignorance and hostility towards the new department as they did not want the expense of paying for it. Clearly we needed more staff and residential services which fitted the needs of the borough. We inherited some residential establishments from the LCC including a vast residential nursery with 300 children under five years of age and a girl's hostel in Brighton. It was horrific and, even after five years, Lewisham Children's Department was not a self-sufficient organization. We finally disengaged ourselves from the Supplies Department and so avoided the situation where every children's home could be immediately recognized by the colour of their sheets or the type of furniture. We introduced local purchasing so that the housemother went out to shop with a child and bought a shirt that fitted.

To begin with we had no remand homes of our own and had to put the girls into Cumberlow Lodge, the huge remand home for girls all over London, and boys into Stamford House. It was not until Lewisham had been going for a couple of years that we managed to get our own remand home.

Another difficulty was that of pay scales. The LCC had paid comparatively well, not only to its child care officers but also to clerical staff. When the LCC staff were transferred to Lewisham, the treasurer said they could not be kept on these scales as they were above what existing Lewisham staff received. We stood our ground and eventually it was resolved. Or car users. The idea that child care officers should need cars as essential not casual users was an anathema to Lewisham. One councillor said, "Why can't they go on a bike to collect parental contributions?"

The councillors, particularly those on the children committee, were eventually co-operative. I had more trouble with the borough treasurer. He could not understand my proposals for more staff and children homes. But I made good relationships with the other departments. The medical officers of health were very helpful while a very friendly architect designed the new children's homes. There was a strong borough co-ordinating committee which met regularly to iron out problems like who was responsible for evicted families.

We inherited a number of old-fashioned child care officers; boarding-out officers, who had come from the early days of the evacuation during the war. They were unqualified and their thoughts were not much beyond receiving a child into care and finding a vacancy. Morale did suffer because of the enormous caseloads, some officers had over 120 cases, and there was a feeling of being over-worked. Then came a number of new, young, keen, well-trained officers so that there was a kind of amalgam between the two types. Clare Marchant was one of the new officers and is now director of social services and housing at Bromley.

The majority of staff were not trained. We then recruited trainees who were sent on courses so that eventually about a third of the child care officers were professionally qualified. Lewisham Children's Department got a good name so that staff wanted to join. But few residential staff were qualified. They had often been there for years. The girl's hostel in Brighton was run by a very elderly couple and one of its features was that it had exactly the same menu every day. For instance, they had tomato soup every day because they got it in large tins from the Supplies Department. The regime for these teenage girls was Dickensian. I altered it immediately. Fortunately, the committee did agree to spend more on small children's homes — for eight to nine children — in Lewisham. By 1968 we had three new homes established in the borough and three being planned. But these became unstuck when the government refused to sanction loans for them.

Over the years changes did occur, particularly in the professional care of children. There was a tremendous drive to obtain more foster parents and for getting them within our own borough rather than poaching them from other areas. One thing that was different from the LCC was that I, as children's officer, could know nearly every child. I made a point of visiting every residential home, no matter how far it was outside of Lewisham, at least once every two months. So apart from those in the nursery, I knew most of the children in the homes.

Over the years we undertook preventative work. Instead of the easy option of taking children into care and putting them into the nearest children's home where there was a vacancy, we did prevention. Each of the five groups of child care officers had a £1,000 to spend on prevention and we only got that out of Lewisham because they realized that prevention was cheaper than residential care. Prevention was one of the achievements of the Lewisham Children's Department. We introduced a family care service where staff went in over-night where, say, a mother was in hospital or had deserted, in order to look after the children. We started a fair amount of community work with the voluntary organizations. We had tremendous help in this respect from the chair of the children's committee, Audrey Callaghan, who was very supportive of our new ideas.

We also pushed forward adoption. In adoption you make a greater change to a child's life than in any other way. I sat on the adoptions panel myself which was unusual for a children's officer. No natural mother ever met the adoptive parents in those days. Children who were adopted never saw their parents again. That has changed now. There has also been a loosening up of the conditions to be an adopter.

We also worked very closely with the juvenile courts. The magistrates were invited to our children's homes and to the department so close links were formed. We set up a specific group of officers to liaise with the courts. The courts made a number of fit person orders and supervision orders to us. The probation service was gradually withdrawing from work with children and concentrating on adults.

In evaluating the work of the Children's Departments, the negative features must be stated. In the LCC because of the enormous strain on residential provision and before fostering was pursued, a number of family members were split apart. On the other hand, children were cared for, clothed and educated far better than they were before 1948. At least the workhouse was gone. Things improved. There was more money around and government was prepared to meet the costs of running Children's Departments. The vast achievement of the departments — in the end, not the beginning — was that families were kept together.

The Children's Departments did throw up some fine leaders. Denis Allen was one. He had experience on the ground before he became a children's officer. He had a certain charisma about him. He was my area children officer when I was a senior. He was always cheerful and bright although he had tragedy in his own personal life. Barbara Drake in the east end of London was a very determined woman who fought committees right and left to get her own way professionally. There were also a number of county women who were children's officers, formidable women but good officers. There was a kind of split between them and the men who were more administratively minded and usually not professionally qualified. In 1971 the Children's Departments came to an end. It was an absurd situation created by the government because they passed the legislation at the very end of the parliamentary session and expected the new Social Services Departments to be up and running within a few months. Local authorities rushed to appoint directors of social services and I went to Bexley until I retired.

Reading back some of the old papers, I am amazed to find that I was a strong supporter of the Seebohm recommendations. I can assure you that after some years I have totally changed my mind. I now think that Seebohm was a disaster — and I am not a lone voice. Many Social Services Departments have now gone back to specialization. How, after the achievement of getting specialist child care officers, we went over to general social workers, I do not know. We also lost the Home Office child care inspectors and the separate child care budget.

Beti Jones

Introduction

Beti Jones was born in 1919 in a mining village in the Rhondda Valley. Her mother was an uncertified teacher, her father a miner. Both were very involved in the community, with the former leading women's groups, and the latter a deacon in the church, a senior St John's Ambulanceman, and the organizer of children's musical concerts. Beti won a scholarship to grammar school and then to university. At the outbreak of war, she registered as a conscientious objector and then taught for two years. From 1943-1947 she was the South Wales organizer for the National Association of Girl's Clubs and helped in a children's home in Cardiff in her spare time. She went as a youth worker to Germany from 1947-1949 under the auspices of the Educational Branch of the British Army of Occupation of the Rhine. She was children's officer of Glamorgan County Council 1949-1968 and director of the Social Work Services Group in the Scottish Office 1968-1987.

Interview

When I was a youth worker in Germany, equipment was desperately short and my old youth club supplied ping pong balls. My mother had my shoes repaired and sent them wrapped in a copy of the *Western Mail*. In it was an advertisement for the children's officer's post in Glamorgan. By now it was 1949 and Glamorgan were a year late in advertising, which was fortunate for me because it stated that the minimum age was 30. To my amazement I got the job.

I could not have had a better authority than Glamorgan. It wasn't that its members had sound knowledge of all child development theories. They had instead an equally important knowledge and understanding and driving force, a warm instinct towards children and a passion to see that their potential was fulfilled. They themselves knew what it was to have their potentials limited by external circumstances. Like the Scots, the Welsh had a passionate belief in the value of education, and were determined that their children should have the best. And that was a pretty good basis on which to begin. I knew nothing of the organization and politics of local government, but I knew and respected the strength of the local communities and their mutual sense of responsibility and their shared passion for justice for children. To this day I am grateful for what the children's committee taught me.

The new children's committee brought together all responsibility for children within the the authority — previously the children's homes had been administered by a separate committee. The Curtis Report and the 1948 Children Act laid down that a local authority should behave like a good parent to the children in its care and the Glamorgan children's committee took that charge seriously. The first chairman was Bill Kedward. A wonderful man, he had been offered a place at Ruskin College but did not take it as he was the sole supporter of his mother. The vice-chair was Alderman Rose

Davies, whose political career had started under Keir Hardie. Both became chairman and chairwoman of the county council in their turn. There were a group of women councillors who had worked in what was called the clerk's committee which had dealt with children who came through the courts. They were highly intelligent women who had busily boarded out children and they brought this experience to the children's committee.

Of course, there were differences. On one occasion I had gone ahead and appointed my own staff. One councillor objected to this and when the matter came up he said, "I won't be defied by a woman." My chairman stuck by me. Yet having a woman in charge accorded with their view of women's roles —the great mother. It would have been more difficult if I had been the chief education officer.

There was the inevitable disappointment when available resources were too limited to allow the change and development at the speed we would have liked. Gradually extra staff were granted and the department was fortunate that Arthur Collis — later professor at Birmingham University — became the first deputy children's officer. He brought a depth of experience and knowledge gained from running the Stepney Family Service Unit throughout the war.

The development of the children's service was parallelled by the expansion of social studies and professional courses in the universities. The links between the Children's Department and the staff at Cardiff University were close and fruitful. Student training was a shared responsibility and professional development opportunities were enjoyed.

This period saw also rapid development in the housing policy of the borough councils and, in time, gave the opportunity to change the pattern of children's homes. The existing pattern was of cottage homes in which there were small estates of six to twelve houses under a housemother, caring for up to twelve boys or girls, with a superintendent and matron overall. The staff were caring but, the children were isolated from the community and were a conspicuous block in the local school. An example of this was that a bus stop was called "children's homes" by the conductors. A more private and intimate pattern was needed and this was undertaken in conjunction with local housing authorities so that we had small homes in the new estates with six to seven children with a housemother and father. The "family" could move in at the same time as other first tenants. The children merged into the local schools, played in the streets with the other children and, most important, brothers and sisters could live together naturally. A great deal of local goodwill was shown. One day at County Hall, I met a lost-looking clergyman. He said, "I have seen an advertisement in the paper for houseparents for a children's home being built in our parish. I'm the curate and I want to be a part of it from the beginning." And he was, and the children were a welcome addition to the church, its choir and nativity plays. There was a wonderful sense of support from the community.

The existence of the Association of Children Officers was an important forum for keeping up to date with developments and debating ideas. Kenneth Brill became the secretary and established the children's officers' *Bulletin* which circulated regularly with news and views. Amongst the notable children's officers were Joan Cooper, Bill Freeman, Lucy Faithfull, Harry Mapstone, Frances Drake. There were some good Welsh ones, Mair Thomas (later Parfitt), Norman Lonsdale, Helen Kegie and Leta Jones. Later, there came a second generation of children's officers like Tom White. The regional group to which I belonged covered the South West of England and South Wales so the links were close with colleagues there. Kenneth Brill was in Devon, Harry Mapstone in Somerset, Dorothy Watkins — warm and imaginative — in Cornwall. The meetings moved around the region and the local chairman attended part so there was a shared enthusiasm with the councillors too.

The Association provided two or three advisers to the County Councils' Association and this became an important channel of influence as we began to evaluate what we were doing. It also made us familiar with the methods elsewhere. While I was adviser to the CCA, I served most of my time with Joan Cooper, Mr Irving of Lancashire and Harry Mapstone. From Joan Cooper I learned the importance of children having a period in a specially staffed reception centre while their needs were being studied so that appropriate longer term arrangements could be made.

In time we were able to develop a reception centre in Glamorgan. With the co-operation of the medical officer of health, we were helped by the consultant child psychtatrist and psychologist from the local hospital. Regular case conferences were held at which the reports of the child care officers, the house staff and the medical and psychological colleagues were considered carefully until the best possible placement was agreed. I chaired them as the person ultimately responsible. and because at this stage of the department's life it was important to show that planning for children was the core of our responsibility. The reception centre was in a pleasant house with a large garden. The gardener was a poet, a crowned bard at the Eistedford. One night I was working late and I saw a movement in the garden. I rushed out thinking it was kids pinching stuff again. It was the gardener and I said, "the county council does not expect you to work these hours." He replied, "Miss Jones, do you take notice of anybody who tells you when to stop work with your children? This is my garden." It was the right kind of ethical standards all around.

Evaluation of the work was making clear that the 1948 Children Act, which authorized care of children, needed amendment to permit helping families in difficulties to prevent separations. The County Councils' Association proved the right forum to discuss this and work towards recommendations for legislation. This was achieved in the Children and Young Persons Act (1963).

Changes in the broader social welfare field were happening too. The National

Institute for Social Work Training was pioneering courses for staff. It became clear that there was a core of knowledge and method necessary for all who worked in the field and, in addition, specialist skills in particular areas like hospital social work, child guidance, child care and work with the disabled and elderly. Courses outside the universities were set-up preparing students for the Certificate of Qualification in Social Work, largely to serve the needs of Welfare Departments. There was a need to try and achieve co-ordination in both training and service delivery and the Seebohm committee was set-up to examine the situation.

My main preoccupation at this time was not the issue of the over-all pattern of social work, important as that was, but how to to solve issues in the child care field which were becoming urgent. Children who had committed an offence were being sent to remand homes to be kept in security until their court hearing. We could see that they needed the reassurance and experience of warm family living and simultaneously some children were being received into care via the 1948 Children Act who were so disturbed that they needed to be kept in security with specialized treatment. It seemed time to deal with the children on the basis of their need not by the route by which they came into care. I was thinking about this at a meeting of the County Councils' Association and making the point that it was no no use sending children to court when what was needed was a helping hand at home. An outraged county clerk broke in and said, "Then what would you do with the young devils who steal my apples?" I summoned my courage and said, "I think I'd want to know if his mother could afford apples."

While all these issues were in the air, the Kilbrandon Report was published in Scotland recommending that any child appearing to need compulsory measures of care should be dealt with by what became known as the children's panels system, a panel of volunteers, who had been chosen and trained for the task, who would examine the situation, receive reports and recommend the method of help which seemed best. I was delighted to speak about it when giving evidence to the Seebohm committee as part of the group from the County Councils' Association. We had to fight to ensure that social workers, not educationalists became directors of the new departments. I remember representing the Association of Children's Officers with Margery Taylor from the Association of Child Care Officers on the same platform as Lord Kilbrandon and making the argument that a background in education departments was not sufficient for the new directors. Education has to concentrate on providing a system of education: the purpose of social work is to achieve growth in individuals, it is a very different focus.

The issues of social work organization in single departments within local authorities and the suggestion of a common training for all social workers continued to be debated. I felt there was a strong case for common basic training but it was essential to provide additional training for the very different groups of workers needed to help people with different patterns of need — e.g. the frail elderly and those with physical disabilities. The issue of recognized professional registration still has not been met.

The re-organization of the personal social services did not get it right. For instance, in Scotland Strathclyde Social Work Department was too big, Argyll was too poor. Communities were lost, members were lost. None the less, having been chief adviser on social work to the Scottish Office from 1968-1987, I can say that skilled heads of departments can sub-divide in order to have several directors under them who can develop specialisms. In addition, having had a number of illnesses, I have come to respect the many ancillary workers now employed by Social Work Departments. I would never have walked again but for physiotherapists.

As the profession of child care nears its fiftieth anniversary and the Social Work Departments and Social Services Departments are beyond their 25th years, the guiding principle must continue to be to evaluate changes in social conditions and personal strains and to develop knowledge and practice to meet needs. Children's Departments carried out the belief that it is every community's responsibility to fulfil a child's potential and to have compensatory schemes where there is a special need. This is a heritage which we must ensure survives.

Barbara Kahan

Introduction
Barbara Kahan was born at Horsted Keynes where her grandfather was a railway station master. She was brought up in a religious and politically left-wing household. From the grammar school she won scholarships to Cambridge University followed by a social science diploma at the London School of Economics. Her first job was an HM Inspector of Factories in the Midlands. She was the first children's officer for Dudley and was children's officer for Oxfordshire 1951-1970. In 1970 she became deputy chief inspector in the Children's Department of the Home Office and held a similar position after amalgamation with the DHSS until1980. From 1980-1991, she directed the Gatsby Project and was chair of the National Children's Bureau 1985-1994. She was professional adviser to the House of Commons Select Committee on Social Services 1983-1990. She worked jointly with Allan Levy QC on the Pindown Inquiry in Staffordshire 1990-1991. Since 1988, she has been an independent consultant and writer.

Interview
While I was HM Inspector of Factories, I read the Curtis Report, wept over it and thought, "This is what I want to do." I went for an interview for the post of children's officer at Dudley. I had no experience except for youth club work in my spare time and, to my amazement, they offered me the job. I was below the minimum age for appointment and Dudley had to get Home Office permission to appoint me.

My appointment dated from 5 July, 1948, the date the Children Act became law. When I arrived, there was just me in a huge room with enormous Public Assistance furniture. On the floor were stacks of files. I had not been in the room for half an hour when an application for reception into care came in. I had no idea what to do. The chairman of the children's committee was a medical practitioner who lived almost opposite so I consulted him.

After six weeks, I got permission to employ a secretary. She was seventeen and very able and motivated. Together for the first nine months we began to work out what the job was about. I had to do everything, visited families, tried to think through the legislation, dealt with the committee members. I hadn't been in the job for more than three months when Pauline Shapiro asked if I would take students from the Birmingham University child care course. I did and later became a regular lecturer there.

I had to change some of the local authority's previous practices. One was that any catholic child was automatically sent to Father Hudson's Homes in Birmingham. With a member of staff, who was a catholic, we made a surprise visit. The nuns were astonished. We were put in a room to wait and the children for whom we were responsible were brought in. One of the little boys had boots which were at least three sizes too big, tied round the ankles with boot laces, and no socks. They were locked out of their dormitories all through the day. It was extremely institutional. I persuaded the children's committee that, in the future, we would not automatically send catholic children to Father Hudson's.

I worked such long hours that after nine months I became ill with double pneumonia. I was desperate to get back to the job. Over two and a half years, I acquired two qualified field workers and two more office staff. One was a very able man from the Factory Department who became our chief clerk. We built up records, a filing system, information material and a working office.

We began to acquire properties for children's homes because the only accommodation apart from foster homes — which had been found by an untrained schools welfare officer — were some cottage homes at Wolverhampton which were used by five county boroughs and where we had twenty places. It was a big, Public Assistance campus with about thirty children in each unit. In my enthusiasm to get to know the children, I visited them quite a lot and obtained agreement to organize outings. So I would turn up at the cottage homes with two or three taxis and go to the zoo or somewhere similar. The children loved it, but on the way home they became totally silent and would run out of the taxis back to their houses without a murmur. Not long after, the children's officer for Wolverhampton wrote to Dudley to request that I should stop the outings as it upset the other children.

We developed a pattern of buying children personal birthday and Christmas presents and of writing them letters. We tried to personalize what we were doing. We moved out of the Public Assistance offices into a house which we bought for a children's home. We had our offices on the ground floor and upstairs — because we had started preventative work — we had a homeless family living. Adolescents in care, who were at a loose end, used to come in at lunch-time and we would cook sausages and fried bread and have a communal lunch with the staff. It was a bit like a settlement and was a wonderful learning experience because the kids relaxed and talked to us in a way they would not have talked in other circumstances.

Dudley had about ninety-five children in care and thirty or so placed for adoption, privately fostered and so on. I wrote a report in which I analysed what we were doing, e.g. how many fostering breakdowns happened because there was not enough accommodation to allow choices; the kind of cases we were dealing with and their outcomes. It helped me formulate what was being done and what needed to be done. The report was circulated widely and I received a very appreciative letter from Eileen Younghusband at LSE. We worked 12-14 hours a day and one of the problems was that there was so little accommodation that sometimes you had to receive a child into care, spend hours ringing around the country to find a spare bed and then have to drive to Nottingham when you found it. On more that one occasion, I — and other staff, including the chief clerk — took children home. I remember one little boy who shared my bed in my rooms in Wolverhampton. He was four or five and was in such an agitated state that my memory is of being kicked in the back all night. We had to improvise.

I started to realize that something was desperately wrong with the way young offenders were treated. I went to the juvenile court myself and I discovered that children were being sent to approved schools for the most trival offences, like stealing a few sticks of rhubarb from a front garden. In one case a white girl of sixteen fell in love with a mixed race boy of seventeen, a nice, responsible boy. The girl's father was so angry that he brought her to court as beyond his control. Despite all our efforts, she was committed to the girls' approved school in Staffordshire. I was determined to go with her and to make it clear to the school that she had friends who wanted to keep in touch and help her. At the school, I made clear my concerns to the headmistress who coldly stated, "Thank you very much, but she is our problem now, not yours. Goodbye." I was so angry I decided that if this was how those rotten places worked then I would do something about it.

Later, I applied to Oxfordshire Children's Department. It was like a bereavement to leave Dudley, but I took it and started on 1st January, 1951 at a salary of £680. In retrospect, I believe they appointed me because they thought they could manage me. The chairman was a railway signalman and I was told by the clerk of the council that if I wanted to talk with him I could go to the signalbox. It was very different from Dudley where committees met in the evening with councillors constantly in touch because they all lived in Dudley. Oxfordshire was a relatively large area fifty miles from one side to another with an earl as the chair of the county council. He nominated the chairs of other committees in a deeply Tory county, the Labour Party was allowed to have anything that was not considered important and my chairman got the children's committee. He gradually got used to me, but it was difficult to be a woman, and a young woman, in local government. I felt I had to make a choice between being a nice girl or a battleaxe. A nice girl they would pat on the head and ignore, while a battleaxe would give them a bit of trouble and they would have to think twice before they dismissed what she said. I had to choose the latter — what else could I do if I wanted to achieve anything?

A few people were kindly disposed towards the children's service but, in the main, it had been forced upon local government and the kinds of attitudes expressed towards it were personified in backward Labour views like, "These kids have had a rough time but so did I and I managed" or those of the aristocracy, one of whom sat on the house committee of a children's home and would say things like, "ice cream! If my children have ice cream for tea I have to pay for it." Awful attitudes. I was filled with detestation for that kind of class distinction and determined to do something for the kids, including getting them well educated.

When I started, there were three fieldworkers, a deputy children's officer and a small office staff. There were seven residential establishments, three of them on one campus in the old Public Assistance style; the others had been purchased quite recently and included two nurseries, a remand home and a long-stay children's home. Two more were opened later. I had to start learning about residential work. I also had to organize a department which had been run by the previous children's officer, a former general practitioner, who was obviously a very warm hearted person but with no administrative experience.

Once in Oxfordshire, I went to the juvenile courts or sent staff who were committed towards our policies, that is, that children before the courts were usually ones who could be helped by a child care service. We had to lay the foundations. We had to write home reports on children which would enable the courts to understand what could he offered. The probation service were doubtful about us. We made friends with the police and encouraged them to feel that if they knew a child who was beginning to go off the rails to refer him/her to us to see what we could or to help. We wanted to avoid children appearing before the courts for, after all, the 1952 Act did give us a legal obligation to try to help them. If they did go to court we tried to avoid them going to approved schools. In the last ten years I was in Oxford there was a six year period in which not a single child went, except one, who was sent by a court in another county. We were able to demonstrate that if they were committed to us they did not come back before the courts. We spent a great deal of time meeting with magistrates, explaining what we were doing so, in the end, they knew and trusted us.

We also tried to make friends with schools and developed regular meetings with the NSPCC and moral welfare workers so they would tell us about their cases and we would exchange information and help. We offered a service to illegitimate children which was not available in most places. This was prevention. In addition, I suspect we saved a lot of pretty haphazard adoptions. Later on we established a regional group including ourselves, other Children's Departments, adoption agencies and moral welfare workers. We pooled information and raised standards of adoption practice. As early as 1960 we ensured that no placements were made without a clear policy of standards concerning visits, information and contacts plus careful scrutiny of the child and the proposed placement by a panel which included not only the people concerned with the child but also others with greater experience. We applied the same standards to fostering so that our breakdown rates were considerably diminished. We used Roy Parker's book *Decision in Child Care* and field workers had to check every proposed placement against his prediction figures as one of the measures used in their assessments.

We gradually became aware of child abuse. It started with physical cruelty. We had professionally well-educated staff and met regularly with child psychiatrists. Gradually it became clear that there was such a thing as non-accidental injury. I remember several cases when something happened to a child and nobody would believe it was non-accidental. One case that made me very aware was when a paediatrician from a local hospital rang to say he had a child who had been placed for adoption. This child had a fractured skull and a former child of the carers, now adopted, had likewise had a fractured skull. The couple concerned were middle class, well known in their area, and had received their babies from a national voluntary society. I went to the police and, after they looked into it, a police inspector rang me to say he was totally convinced that it was accidental and that the woman had tripped over the front-door step and dropped the baby. That was the end of any police action. I then went to the adoption agency and told them what the doctor had said and asked them to remove the child. They were very resistant but in the end they agreed. An astonishing sequel was that a couple of years later the husband came to ask us to place a child with them. In the end, I told him we would never do so and if they got one from anywhere else and it came before a court in Oxford, I would do my best to prevent an adoption being made.

We had regular meetings with the NSPCC and encouraged health visitors and teachers to refer cases of neglect and ill-treatment to us. From 1952, we had a full-time former Family Service Unit worker who did nothing else but families of this kind with a caseload of 10-11. We would try to see if the ill-treatment was due to stress, illness, poverty, or whatever and then see how we could modify it. In some cases we had to get a doctor involved, and deal with it as a case of cruelty. Some children we had to remove but most we tried to keep at home. In one case, while I was in Dudley, the NSPCC took a case of neglect to court when a mother had a baby in conditions of squalor. The baby came into care with the couple's other child. I had another former FSU worker in

Dudley and he went to see them and, based on his considerable experience, he said they were not cruel parents. The husband was partially blind, the woman was not very skilled and he thought they were vulnerable human beings having to cope with too much. He did an enormous amount to help them, raised money and persuaded them that the husband should bring his wages every week to the office, so that we could work with them and give them a certain amount every day. Over time we restored the children to them and, after a while, the health visitor said their standards were as good as anyone else's in the area. In Oxfordshire we developed similar methods of prevention and it spread throughout the department.

Today physical cruelty and neglect seems to have gone into the background while sexual abuse is prominent. Sexual abuse had not really surfaced by the time I left Oxfordshire. What had surfaced was the knowledge that parents could deliberately damage their children. There were cases of incest but we probably missed other sexual abuses. Several years ago two sisters came to see me. Both had been in the care of Oxfordshire, one received before I went there. One told me that as a young teenager she had been put in a foster home with a policeman and his wife. She was terrified of this man because every time the wife went out she had to lock herself in the bathroom for safety. She said it took months to persuade the fieldworker that anything was wrong. The other sister was in children's home. The couple in charge were trained and ran a very peaceful and supportive home. Relatives of theirs used to visit and eventually the girl was fostered with them. Not long afterwards she made a suicide attempt and came back to the children's home where she thrived. She told me that she attempted suicide to attract attention because every time she had a bath the husband tried to get her on his lap and she feared what would happen. I asked why she did not tell us and she said, "would anyone have believed me?" I had to admit we probably would have found it very difficult.

When I went to Oxfordshire, there were just under 400 children in care; when I left there were about 500. I am not ashamed of that. Jean Packman's study *Child Care Needs and Numbers* arose from many efforts by the local authority to prove that the Oxfordshire department was doing things the wrong way. In the end I suggested a research study and it demonstrated that you could not tell why the numbers in care varied so greatly just by looking at figures. Recently I wrote that it now seems politically desirable to have low numbers in care and that this is believed to demonstrate good practice. In my view, it depends on whether they need to be in care or not and there is no evidence I know of that demonstrates statistically one way or the other.

I had a pretty fraught life as a result of having high numbers in care. One investigation after another took place all the time. The local authority started with the finance committee; then they got the Home Office inspectors to do a special investigation. The inspectors told them they had got a very good service. They then put an Organisations and Methods investigator in. He came for a month and arrived at findings like "if the children's officer receives forty-five illegitimate children into care in a year then she should place forty-five children for adoption." I remember staying up all night writing responses which, in the end, fought off this ridiculous report. The final attempt was a special finances and general purposes committee run by the chair of the finance committee who had been an administrator in India. In the end he gave up too.

In 1970 when it was clear there were going to be changes, the job of deputy chief inspector in the Home Office Children's Department was advertised. I sent for the forms and received those for a government agricultural post. Then Joan Cooper sent me the right forms and eventually I was offered the job but I was not sure. My husband, who had been a tower of strength, urged me to go though I would have enjoyed being a director of social services. The clerk of the county indicated that while I was highly regarded I spent too much money and was unlikely to be appointed. So I went to the Home Office.

The Children's Departments as a whole turned a minimalist Public Assistance service into a much more personalized and child-centred service. The whole pattern of children's homes changed. Fostering became a much more flexible and wide ranging service. Children were treated much more like children in their own homes so that, for example, it became customary for them to be as well-dressed as anyone else's children and any suggestion that they should not be well-fed or properly looked after according to normal parental standards was anathema. We managed to get rid of the concept that children coming in care were servant fodder for the well-to-do or obvious recruits for the army or as farm workers. Children had regular holidays, pocket money and the treats that other children had. It became like ordinary family standards. In many departments, children with abilities were encouraged and in Oxfordshire they might receive music or riding lessons or similar extras.

We brought children and parents back together and managed as much as possible to keep siblings together. We were saying, "Here is a child whom the law says is entitled to be treated like everybody else's child and this is what we are going to do." This is not to deny that much remained to be done by 1970 and services varied in standards between and within departments. There were things we did not achieve. It was still common for school teachers to see children in care as being something quite different. I think they often still do and children in care get excluded much more readily. But the Children's Departments did have a great influence on the course of child care generally and on developments like Seebohm.

The Children's Departments were driven by hard-working and motivated staff. The child care officers were well educated, they knew the law, they were systematic. It has never been easy to get social workers to keep good records but they were kept better than now. Many child care officers were attracted to work with children. The task of trying to compensate children for what they had lost fell in nicely with a feminine approach to life for many of the early officers were women. Social work could still be fairly evangelistic and not be ashamed of being so. There was a climate of targeted intention to achieve as much as possible which tended to get lost after 1970. In most departments, the child care officers were near enough to the senior staff to know what the objectives of the department were, to identify with them and develop a sense of unity with the whole department.

Amongst the outstanding children's officers, I would name Bill Freeman who had a strong sense of motivation and who saw child care as a campaign. Kenneth Brill and I sometimes took exception to what each other said, but he was outstanding as someone prepared to put heart, soul and ability into the work. So was Sylvia Watson. Ian Brown of Manchester really worked hard at achieving what the 1948 Children Act set out to do and stuck doggedly with the research set up by the Association of Children's Officers that showed fostering was being over played and needed to be more discriminating.

On behalf of the Association of Children Officers, I wrote much of the evidence for the Seebohm committee. Initially we wanted Seebohm to bring all the children's services together — the Children's Departments along with school welfare from education and other children's services from health and probation — and then allow some time before the rest of the adult services were brought in. But some members of the Seebohm Committee were strongly opposed and in the end the children's officers accepted that it should all happen at once. Looking back, I think it may have been a mistake because child care got totally swamped. The other sad thing was that the Children and Young Persons Act (1969), which was a logical development from the work of the Children's Departments, got washed away by Seebohm and local government reorganization.

After 1970 our vision of child care went out of the window. Today I am deeply concerned at some of the things which happen. Children in care now have numerous changes of placements and separation of siblings has been much too common. The experience of Pindown in Staffordshire demonstrated some of the things that have happened in residential work. Pindown could thrive there because so many homes had been closed and what were left were expected to do everything with no extra resources. That seems to have been a pattern elsewhere as well.

The organization of Social Services Departments going generic overnight was ill-conceived. It would have been better to have had a federation of social workers with specialists and some generalists but not to give everybody mental health, the elderly, delinquents, adoption. What better method could you have found to destroy something? Directors of social services have been at a height so far removed from the coal face that they have not been able to know what was going on in their departments.

Large organizations seem to have been less able to replicate the relatively firm corporateness of senior staff and practitioners working together with common standards and purposes as Children's Departments experienced. Everything seems so fragmented and good child care can not be done in a fragmented way.

What is so sad about the present situation is that so many staff seem to have no real sense of conviction about what can be achieved with children and young people. They have a feeling of working hard yet in some of my consultancy work I have found foster children amongst unallocated cases even when caseloads were as low as 15-20 per worker. The hands-on staff often do not receive the professional supervision and support they need in the extremely difficult work they have to do whether in group care or in field work. Social work seems to have become more a job than a vocation. And there is a lack of leadership. It is very discouraging to see what has happened.

Social work is among those occupations in which stress has greatly increased. I can only hope that with a change of political climate we may recover some of the optimism which is needed in such a difficult task.

Alfred Leeding

Introduction
Alfred Leeding was born in 1910 near Sheffield and, after a settled childhood, worked as a clerk for Sheffield Corporation while he also took the university external diploma in public administration. In 1934, he was accepted as a trainee probation officer in Manchester. He moved as a probation officer to East Sussex until the war took him abroad in the armed forces. From 1944-1947, the Home Office seconded him to set-up a probation service in Ceylon. He returned to probation in Eastbourne but was so stimulated by the Curtis Report that he obtained the post of assistant children's officer in the Gloucestershire Children's Department. From 1958-1971 he was the children's officer in Warwickshire. After retiring, he took the post of research officer in Gloucestershire Social Services Department until 1976.

Interview
I went to Warwickshire in 1958 in somewhat awkward circumstances. The former children's officer had been demoted after some questions were asked in Parliament about a girl in care. Warwickshire had 600 children in care, covered six sizable boroughs as well as the rural areas, but had only six child care officers plus another responsible for adoptions. They were all women, none professionally qualified. They worked so hard and once, after the Home Officer inspector told me they were the best in the Midlands, I felt so proud of them. They were nearly all religious people and I think that was their driving force. Gradually the numbers of child care officers were increased and, at the end, we had 20 but we were still understaffed. Warwickshire was not a fashionable county like Somerset or Devon and we had difficulties in recruiting qualified staff.

The council was made up mainly of Independent councillors who were really Conservative but political divisions were not great. The children's committee was old fashioned and I was fortunate that its chairman, Mr Sheperdson, was open to my ideas and supportive to me in trying to get them through the committee.

My initial task was to break down what I called the Homes Empire. At Warwick there was a semicircle of children's homes comprising six identical homes for twelve children each plus a nursery. A seventh, slightly bigger home, was inhabited by the superintendent and matron with a girl in care as "the maid". The superintendent oversaw all the other children's homes in the county and had an office, two clerks, a large garden with three gardeners. Outside was an enormous flagpole in memory of the alderman who planned this children's village and it was the council's intention to complete the circle by building six more establishments in order to accommodate all children in residential care in Warwickshire.

I disliked the bringing all children together and the centralization with all the children's homes in the county having to send to the superintendent for food, clothes, even electric light bulbs. Food came from a wholesaler, clothes were bought in bulk. I gradually liberalized the residential regime. I gave the houseparents the power to buy their own supplies. Gradually the superintendent's position was phased out. Then I got smaller homes run by married couples and the intention to complete the circle was withdrawn. I was in the children's homes a lot and I think some of the children turned to me as a kind of father figure.

I also wanted to improve the child care officers' contacts with children. A family in Nuneaton would be received into care, some put into a home or nursery, others boarded-out wherever there was a foster home. It might be in Leamington or Solihull or even in Worcestershire but wherever it was the child care officer in that area would supervise the children not the one who had received them into care. It was system of fragmentation which had scant regard for keeping children in contact with each other and made rehabilitation more difficult. I changed this to give the "home" child care officer responsibility for the whole family and ultimately instituted a system of reviews in which all members of a family were looked at the same time, instead of separately. All the time we were developing boarding-out, although it never reached the levels of some departments. I always had some ambivalence about boarding-out and did not think it should be pursued to the cost of everything else. I always thought there was a place for residential care. For children who were to return home, it was sometimes preferable to be in a home which was near to their parents.

I inherited an adoptions officer who was very good and had arranged adoptions for children in care. The medical officer of health still ran a mother and baby home but, after the 1958 Children Act, we arranged the adoptions of the babies from there as well. But there were aspects of adoption which made me uneasy such as the drastic effects of an adoption order. Also I was uneasy about the vogue for "matching", making sure the baby had the same colour eyes as the prospective adopters, as this only encouraged adopters to claim they were the real parents. It was far more important to make sure that the potential adopters and natural parents knew as much as possible about each other. When the adoptions officer left, we appointed Peter Brown and tried out some different approaches. We invited anyone who expressed interest in adoption to a meeting that explained adoption. As a result some decided it was not for them. The remainder were invited to further meetings where they could meet adopted people and a few adopters to learn from their experience. Later we were more radical and involved the natural parents and prospective adopters in meeting each other and even in continued contact after adoption. Some of this brought outraged comments from some of the Midland adoption agencies. I wanted to undertake a survey of adoptions which the department had arranged in order to assess the outcomes. However, the children's committee would not give permission on the grounds that adoption was final. At least we were insistent that single mothers should know about their rights to keep their children. I think we improved adoption.

We were also responsible for supervising private fosterings, Child Life Protection as it was called. It was a submerged problem and we used to put notices in post offices telling private foster parents of their duty to inform us if they took children. If they had done so it would have meant much more work for us. Certainly, some private foster children would have been better off in care and, in extreme cases, we did intervene.

The Children and Young Persons Act (1963) brought new challenges. It gave sanction to preventative work which had been going on in some places for years. I was keen to use the powers under the act to stop unhelpful admissions to care and to return children to their parents. All local charities were listed and used. Help with bedding and furniture was provided for struggling families. Child care officers and police shared views before juveniles were prosecuted. The committee was wary and the clerk of the county council referred to prevention as "a bottomless pit." I did not allow staff to spend cash on paying overdue electric or gas bills. Of course, prevention could go too far and later the Colwell case was about a child who should have stayed in care and was returned to a hopeless mum. None the less, we did succeed in returning home some children who should not have been kept in care — like twelve children from one family who stayed for years after their parents had a housing difficulty. I used to shut myself away and go through all the names of children in care to see what could be done. I was pressing the child care officers all the time to return them.

When I started I was still an innocent about the job. I got help from two sources. One was the Home Office Inspectorate. The other was The Association of Children's Officers which sent out very informative circulars. When I was first appointed I went to see Harry Mapstone, whom I admired very much, in Somerset. Leslie Turner was very helpful as was Jim Chaplin of Birmingham. I then went to the meetings of the Midlands branch of the association and met others and eventually became its secretary.

In 1964 I was asked to give some lectures on law to child care students at Birmingham University. I prepared notes for the students and they were well received. This made me think there was a need for a book on the legal basis for child care work. It was published by Butterworths and Leeding's Child Care Manual went to four editions. I was grateful to Kenneth Brill who wrote to me to say "All child care is in your debt."

In 1969, with the reorganization looming, I decided to retire. The county appointed the chief welfare officer as the new director of social services and persuaded me to stay on to the end of the year to deal with child care matters. After my retirement I took a post with Gloucestershire Social Services Department until retiring properly in 1976.

I knew that Children's Departments were too small but I had thought that the way to proceed was to join it with parts of education to form a new children's service and then to add other services at a later stage. More radically, I thought that children's work could have been taken out of local government altogether and put under a national body akin to the National Health Service. There were terrible inequalities between local authorities so the Children's Departments varied enormously in their resources and in their leadership. A national body could have over-ruled this. The Seebohm Report did refer to a group of social workers who argued "clearly and forcefully" that personal social services should cease to be local authority functions. But this was outside the committee's terms of reference.

Today's Social Services Departments have not got the commitment that we had, certainly not the commitment to children. There is nothing like the crusading zeal that started in 1948. It was just after the war, we all thought we were building a better world. The Children's Departments were like a missionary enterprise. Now a good deal of high level time seems to be concerned with reorganization. One pattern follows another, changing more rapidly even than the personnel, and paper rules supreme. I can say that as a children's officer I took no part in pressing for higher salaries and was content with what I had. Today major concerns seem to be salaries and promotion with managers removed from the grass roots, dwelling in some land whose language of Newspeak I find incomprehensible. I am glad to say that I have a daughter with thirty years experience in social work who has declined promotion and is happy to get on with the job — as far as they will let her.

John Moorwood

Introduction

Born in 1915 in Sheffield, John Moorwood's father was a hairdresser with his own small shop. On leaving school, John worked for the Sheffield Corporation's Printing Department as a bookbinder. Influenced by Quakers, he became a conscientious objector and during the second world war worked in two approved schools, the second being the famous Aycliffe School. In 1952, John and his wife went as superintendent and matron of a working boys' hostel with Nottingham Children's Department. In 1958, John Moorwood took a post as a child care officer with Burnley Children's Department and was its Children's Officer from 1964-1971. After the reorganization of the personal social services, he was deputy director of the Burnley Social Services Department and then, following local government reorganization, was deputy divisional director in Lancashire Social Services Department until his retirement in 1975.

Interview

I came to Burnley as a child care officer in 1958 when Marion Jones was the children's officer. After her death in 1961, I took over as acting children's officer until the new man, Harry Bassett, was appointed. In 1962, I was seconded to the National Institute for Social Work Training where I was taught by Eileen Younghusband and David Jones on a course which gave us a professional qualification in generic social work. At the end, and as part of the course, I did a project in Burnley about fostering. We had worked hard to increase the number of children in foster homes but I had observed the high rate of foster parent drop outs. My study pinpointed some of the reasons — disappointments, frustrations, not getting the right children, finding them too difficult and so on. Harry Bassett left to go onto the inspectorate and I was appointed children's officer in 1964.

When I took over, the department had just four child care officers, one children's home and about ninety children in care. It also dealt with juvenile court work, adoption, and supervision of boys and girls released from approved schools. Pressure for expansion came with the Children and Young Persons Act (1963) giving us responsibilities for prevention. The children's committee were usually ready to expand. The chairman was a strong socialist, very outspoken, who refused to wear evening dress at official functions. He was very astute and very friendly towards me. If I proved I needed an extra member of staff, he would fight to get it through and usually succeeded. This was sometimes despite the opposition of the treasurer and town clerk who used to take the line that parents should look after their own children and not cost the rates anything. But those were the days when the Home Office contributed a large grant towards any Children's Department expenditure so that made it easier.

Our staff grew to seven child care officers and a part-time adoptions officer. One of the unqualified child care officers, a teacher, was Deryk Mead. He was brilliant and later became a director of social services and is now chief executive of NCH Action for

Children. They were a contented and closely knit team and I am still in touch with most of them. The new Act meant an increase in family casework with families where children might come into care. We appointed a family caseworker to co-ordinate this although each child care officer carried some cases of this kind. We also opened three new children's homes run by a housemother with a husband who went out to work. It might seem strange to open homes at a time when the emphasis was on fostering and prevention. But Burnley had a number of children placed with voluntary agencies, particularly catholic children or large families which we wanted to keep together. This meant that our officers were always travelling to Bury, Blackpool, Preston, Manchester etc., to these homes and also it meant that the children were not near their own parents. So we opened these additional establishments and gradually moved the children back to Burnley. The residential staff were unqualified but they did pretty well.

I also wanted to improve adoption. Apart from the adoption of children in our care, adoption was mainly conducted by voluntary organizations and I found these too restrictive in that they were religiously-based or would not take mixed marriages or put limits on the ages of prospective adopters. I wanted an agency which would place a greater range of children with a greater range of adopters. We set Burnley ourselves up as an adoption agency, but we were too small so that children from Burnley were likely to be placed with adopters from Burnley with the greater chance that their paths would keep crossing afterwards. So I drew in a number of other small Children's Departments, Bury Blackpool, Blackburn and Bolton to join us. We then had a panel of prospective adopters and so could place Burnley children in their areas and vice versa.

Today you read about the lack of communication between different services yet we set-up an 'at risk' register and the family care worker liaised with the various local authority departments. I had a meeting every month with other agencies — probation, health visitors, the police, welfare officers, housing officials, NSPCC and so on — in which we pooled information about children at risk, decided what help was required and which service was appropriate to supervise. Of course, some agencies still had to go in because of statutory obligations but it did reduce some duplication of visiting. It made a lot of work because there were so many cases and it made for long meetings. But, in other ways, it saved work.

Again, there was good co-operation between children's officers. The Association of Children's Officers had a branch in the north-west which I went to regularly. It was particularly important in my early days when I needed advice. Ian Brown of Manchester was very approachable and I also remember that he came here to chair a day conference which I organized about fostering and which included foster parents. The children's officers became a close-knit group. Marjorie Decker of Preston and Bill Irving of Lancashire stand out in my mind.

Then came the Seebohm Report and the amalgamation of Children's Departments into Social Services Departments. At the time I could see some of the arguments for reform. A larger department would mean more facilities: a Social Services Department would have wider acceptance than small Children's Departments. But I also saw the arguments against. Small Children's Departments like Burnley did have some advantages: I knew all the children in our care and all the families: I was known to and accessible to the child care officers and when they came to discuss a family I knew who they were talking about. Once I moved into a Social Services Department I sat in an office and something was missing. And the former child care officers, then social workers, complained that they did not see me, but had to discuss cases with intermediary managers who did not know the families.

Reorganization went over the top. I was never a great believer in generic casework. There was a view that the good social worker should be able to do the same casework with the elderly, children, the mentally ill etc. At the start of the Social Services Departments we were expected to give social workers a balance of different kinds of clients yet those from mental health backgrounds were soon complaining that they could not cope with child care legislation, former child care officers said that they did not understand adult mental ill-health and so on. So they got frustrated and lost enthusiasm. I hear that now there is a move back to greater specialization.

Another loss was the end of the Home Office child care inspectorate. The inspectors, based in Manchester, were always ready to come and give advice. Their inspections also kept staff on their toes. They looked at files and asked questions about families. They went with child care officers to visit foster homes, they inspected children's homes and made a thorough inspection of the administration. When it became a Social Services inspectorate all this seemed to go. The closeness between inspectors and field officers was lost, and this was a mistake. One of the great contributions of the Children's Departments was that they put training on the map and produced far more qualified social workers than the Welfare Departments. This was partly due to the Home Office pushing training and providing resources.

I must be careful not to be too critical of Social Services Departments. They have had far more duties piled upon them. And society has changed, it is probably far more aggressive and anti-social than it was. And Social Services Departments are forced to make changes. They now do much less providing of services and have to direct clients towards private or voluntary residential homes.

It is useful to remember why Children's Departments came into being. The inquiry into the death of Dennis O'Neill found that the involvement of varying departments meant that visiting was mixed up and children neglected. The Curtis Report concluded that when varying local authority services — health, education, public assistance — looked after deprived children then none of them did it properly. It concluded that a separate department just for deprived children was required, a department that had no other encumbrances. It was right. The creation of Children's Departments was an enlightened step and it worked out well. It meant there was a local authority committee which concentrated just on children: those committees reviewed every child every six months, child care officers had to write reports about their progress with families and committee members read them. After Seebohm all this was lost. The 1948 Children Act had meant that in the children's officer there was one official who was responsible for the children. It was a success. But with the advent of Social Services Departments and the introduction of generic case loads much of the intimacy and dedication towards the care of children was lost. I have every sympathy with the social workers of today, whose work has become so widened and diverse and is in full glare of a rather hypercritical press.

John Murphy

Introduction
John Murphy was born in East Stirlingshire in 1917, a few months after his father was killed in the battle of Ypres. After school and a degree in classics at Glasgow University, he completed teacher training at Jordanhill College in 1939. With the outbreak of war he joined the army and spent some time on the staff of the War Office Selection Board where he worked with John Bowlby. After the war, John and his wife taught at a residential school before he joined the Home Office inspectorate in 1950 as an inspector of child care. In 1961, he went to the Scottish Education Department as an inspector of approved schools. From 1959 to 1975 he was director of social work with Stirling County and then for the new Central Region until 1978. From 1979 to 1982 he served as a Commissioner for Mental Welfare in Scotland.

Interview
When I joined the Home Office inspectorate, the chief inspector was Elaine Scorrer, a great and able woman who knew how to handle the chairmen of counties and county boroughs. She had considerable influence with administrative secretaries in the Home Office. The Under Secretary of State was John Ross, a concerned man who had been disabled in the first world war.

In England, the years 1950-1960 were a great child care crusade. It was ably led by a bunch of outstanding graduate women as children's officers. In addition, there was a powerful, interested and concerned inspectorate at the Home Office. The growth was initially on the residential side. Large children's homes were split up and new ones opened. Another influence in the first decade was training. It was perceived in England at an early stage that training was essential. Before the Curtis Report was even out, a move had been made towards training on the residential side. The Central Training Council in Child Care was founded in 1947 led by an outstanding woman, Sybil Clement Brown so that, by the end of the 1950s, trained child care officers were coming off courses in plenty. Also, the first generic course was set up in 1954 at the LSE and it produced some outstandingly able young officers.

The emphasis for the first five to six years was on residential work. There was not boarding-out on the same scale as in Scotland which had a long tradition of fostering. In the mid 1950s, the Home Office began getting cold feet about the expense of the new system and took notice of Scotland where fostering was cheaper. So circulars came from the Home Office promoting boarding-out. This was the picture at the end of the first decade.

It would be wrong to suggest that all was sunshine and progress. There were very progressive authorities in the Home Counties. Around Tyneside, boroughs like Gateshead, Hartlepool and Middlesborough did not develop services so well. I have memories of the cottage homes in Middlesborough where one housemother, with an occasional relief, coped with thirty boys. Again, in some of the ultra rural areas down the east coast in Lincolnshire, North Riding and East Riding, committees were squirearchical who did not spend the money on this new service. Generally, there was great progress in child care in England with patches which were not so good.

Towards the end of the 1950s, some of the really thinking children's officers were realizing the basic defect of the 1948 Children Act, that taking children into care and providing substitute homes was not as good as dealing with the families in the first instance. Family work was beginning to develop in places like Oxfordshire, Hertfordshire and Kent but this ran into legal and financial problems. The Children and Young Persons Act (1963) marked some progress, especially with its Section 1 which definitely allowed Children's Departments to move into preventative work with families. The Ingelby Report which led to the 1963 Act also contained ideas about a move into a family service alongside proposals for reforming the juvenile courts. England looked longingly at Scandinavia with its juvenile panel systems but it was never achieved despite various White Papers. The Ingelby Report could be summed up in Horace's words, "The mountains heaved in labour and a ridiculous mouse was born". The ensuing Children and Young Persons Act (1969) settled nothing. It also left a lot of dissatisfaction within the approved schools. In the 1950s, approved schools in England and Wales, under the inspiration of figures like John Gittins, had developed classifying systems, vocational training and rehabilitative work with families. They lost many of their distinguishing features in 1969.

In 1961, I moved to Scotland as an inspector of approved schools which came under the Scottish Education Department. Here I saw the failure of the Scottish Children's Departments to provide adequate residential care so that often the children finished up in the approved schools. But the approved schools in the 1950s were very old fashioned. The drive during the 1960s was to modernize the approved schools, to split up the great barrack places, to develop house units on the lines set down by John Gittins, and to set in motion training for staff. We managed to obviate corporal punishment in approved schools before it happened in the ordinary Scottish schools. Scotland did not have classifying schools but the approved schools system did have a clutch of psychologists who went around the schools working with the heads and staff. So the 1960s did see a jump forward in altering regimes. In 1969 I was involved in opening six new schools. Many had trained staff who could cope better with difficult children than children's homes. They were a valuable asset but by this time the climate of opinion had turned against them so this valuable resource was pretty well thrown away. The leaders in thought in child care and social work were hostile to them and they trained a new generation of students who took the same attitudes. Under Social Work Departments, approved schools were relegated to being List D schools.

What of the Scottish Children's Departments? For the first 15 years following 1948, Scotland was a backward service. The 1948 Children Act was not seized upon with enthusiasm in Scotland. The Scottish Office attitude, as can be seen in the Clyde Report of 1946, was that everything was alright in Scotland and it was only in England and Wales that matters had gone wrong as shown in the O'Neill tragedy. The powerful people in Scotland, particularly directors of education who had been responsible for the operation of the Children and Young Persons (Scotland) Act (1937) saw no need for change. It was also the attitude of the chief inspector of child care, William Hewitson Brown (who had been the secretary of the Clyde Committee). He was a dominating influence in the Scottish Home Department and had a direct line to its permanent secretary, Charles Craig Cunningham, to whom he sold the virtues of Scottish boarding out and the message not to trouble this. To many local authorities, the Children's Departments were unnecessary and an expensive innovation. The Curtis Committee had said that 400 children was a sufficient number to justify a children's officer. In Scotland, only Glasgow, Edinburgh, Aberdeen and Dundee could muster that figure. Even Dundee with 450 children, appointed just a children's officer and one assistant. The Scottish Office tried to get some authorities to make joint arrangements but they would not: they preferred to have part-time children's officers or to let the welfare officer also carry the post. There were few Scottish professional associations at that time. One was the Scottish Association of Welfare Officers and it went to the Scottish Home Department to say that it did not see the case for employing such high calibre women, as specified by Curtis, and suggested that men be children's officers with a few women as assistants. The Association of Child Care Officers, in one of their publications, summed it up well by saying, "initially child care in Scotland was a depressed service, starved of resources both money and professional, and that there was a tendency for officers to travel south for training, better jobs and salaries."

The other factor that killed development in Scotland was the lack of training. The Advisory Committee on Child Care only got this going in the 1960s and even then it produced few officers because numbers were small and there was a lack of qualified child care officers to take on as tutors. Of the fifty-two children's officers in Scotland, it is doubtful if fifteen had a qualification of any kind. And this in a country which is qualification orientated. The council would have a clerk with a law degree, an education officer and medical officer of health with degrees and professional qualifications. Children's officers were of low status by comparison.

Then things changed in two directions. One was the transfer in 1960 of the responsibility for child care from the Scottish Home Department to the Scottish Education Department. Bob Corner had become chief inspector of child care and probation. He was a former school master and colonel with the characteristics of Stalin. He was recruited from the Home Office inspectorate and he discovered how backward things were in Scotland. He tried to get rid of the dead wood in the inspectorate, promoted new blood and upped the standards. An able administrator also emerged in Jim Johnston who became an assistant secretary. The other factor was the revival of the Scottish Advisory Council on Child Care under the chairmanship of Catherine Tennant, Lady Elliot, who had been the chair of the Roxburghshire children's committee. It produced a series of reports on remand homes, the McBoyle Report on *The Prevention of Neglect of Children*, and, most important, *Staffing of Local Authority Children's Departments* in 1963. If there was a golden age of Scottish child care it was 1964-1969. During this period, able trained people like Vera Hiddleston, Julia Robertson and Dick Poor assumed leading roles in Children's Departments such as Midlothian, Angus and Stirling County. A number of children's officers and staff were striving to raise standards. Even so, Glasgow with over 3,000 children in care had only half the number of child care officers as Oxfordshire.

For a decade, England had been talking about change. Scotland suddenly seized the idea that progress had to be made. It is often top civil servants who make or break ideas and, at this period, Scotland had some great ones. Down south the Oxbridge civil servants were often dilettante and distant. In Scotland, there were civil servants from Scottish schools and universities who knew what was happening and were close to the minister. David Cowperthwaite was assistant secretary at the Scottish Home Department and was very much in agreement with Jim Johnston at the Scottish Education Department. They were interested in both juvenile justice and social work. The Kilbrandon Committee was set up in 1961 with an outstanding chairman, able committee membership, enlightened civil servants and the political will of the minister, Judith Hart. When it reported in 1964, Judith Hart — product of LSE, socialist, social theorist — was determined that it would be acted upon. In 1965 she appointed three experts to advise on the creation of Children's Hearings and Social Work Departments. They were Richard Titmuss of LSE, Megan Browne of Edinburgh University, and Kay Carmichael of Glasgow University. The outcome was the Social Work (Scotland) Act (1968). Kilbrandon started after the Ingelby Report yet the legislation came two years before the English act. Juvenile courts had never taken hold in Scotland so there was a welcome for the new system of Children's Hearings. The Children's Departments were abolished and integrated into the Social Work Departments in 1969.

The Scottish Children's Departments had achieved an awareness of the child care problem, that it was not sufficient to export masses of children from the cities to the Highlands and Islands. They established a need for smaller children's homes and this was accepted by the great voluntary societies, Quarriers, Aberlour, Nazareth House and others, so progress was made in breaking down their size.

But the change to Social Work Departments was timely and right. Energy was concentrated on child care and families. The speciality which suffered was probation — it remained a separate service in England. But directors of social work were much more seen as chief officers than children's officers had been. Some very able directors were recruited, a number from England such as Maurice Speed, Jim Gregory and Fred Edwards. Staff were enthusiastic and not as isolated as before.

There is no doubt that departments became larger and probably more bureaucratic. Small scale authorities to tend to be well run but often they lacked sufficient resources for a range of services. Strathclyde was an enormous authority but it had the capacity to think strategically about problems and could move resources around. Also it was able to extract resources from the Scottish Office and from European funds.

Dick Poor

Introduction
Dick Poor was born in 1925 in Sheffield. His father died when Dick was young and he was brought up in Bristol where he was much influenced by a church youth club. He attended WEA courses at Fircroft College and, in 1951-53, studied at Barnet House, Oxford intending to do youth work. However, he then undertook the child care course, at Liverpool University and while on a student placement he met his future wife — his supervisor! After working for Lancashire Children's Department for ten years, Dick moved to Scotland to become children's officer for Stirling County in 1964. With the creation of Social Work Departments, he became director of Argyll and, after local government reorganization, the deputy director in Lanarkshire until his retirement in 1986.

Interview
Lancashire Children's Department was progressive and lively. The children's officer was Horace Robert Irving and the staff included Ted Brown, Barry Newall, Margaret Fryars and Helen Seed. I started at Wigan as a child care officer and later moved to Bury as an area officer. It was a good grounding for when I moved to Scotland in 1964.

Stirling Children's Department was small with only five field staff and no deputy children's officer. My predecessor was Sandy McDonald, a kindly and highly regarded character and I was able to build on his reputation. The staff had no professional training except one who had done a Younghusband course. As children's officer, I still personally took children into care and did out-of-hours stints. The staff were youngish people, committed. Morale was high. In the end I did get some trained staff, including Ian Gilmour who moved from the welfare service. Scotland had fifty-two Children's Departments so there were many minnows. The children's officers were good people, reliable but paternalistic. Stirling had 300-400 children in care. It only ran one children's home of its own, Weedings Hall in Polmont. Most children in residential care were placed with voluntary societies. One of my early lessons was that you had to go at least once a year to find out what was happening in these children's homes. You could not assume that it would be the same as three years before.

In Lancashire there had been a drive on boarding out, we looked up our position in the league table and poured over a weekly publication that came round showing which children were available for fostering. In Scotland that did not happen. Fostering was more akin to quasi-adoption with children placed out in the Highlands and Islands. There was a tradition of councillors visiting them once a year with the child care officers — the visitation. In England they visited children's homes but not foster homes. I did not like it. The councillors were uncomfortable and didn't know what to do. But I think the foster parents enjoyed it. A limitation was that you never saw the child's bedroom and never saw the child alone. One of my tasks was to change this, to explain to foster parents why you had to do it without losing their trust. Many of these foster homes were outside the county but Scotland does have the advantage that you can go anywhere and return in a day. So, if necessary, you could reach a child quickly. Basically I did not like these quasi-adoption fosterings. Families were broken up and children were not kept in touch with their parents or with each other. There were justifiable anxieties about these fosterings when children were boarded out well away from our county. It could be difficult to contact the local district nurse or teacher if you wanted information. I know that some of those foster children might say they enjoyed it but I do not think these kinds of fosterings were the best for them. The children were removed from environments which had been familiar to them and from their families to live with foster parents who tended to be kind but not loving. In the end, once out of care, the children nearly always made their way back to their own parents.

The first chairman of the children's committee was a very learned minister who taught me a great deal. He used to enjoy coming with me to different places and had a breadth of life experience that was invaluable. He was very forthright, had a number of enemies, and was a good chairman. He was succeeded by various ladies who were interested and committed. But the status of the children's committee was low compared with other committees in the authority. If you kicked up a fuss if children were coming into care because their parents were being evicted, they wondered what you were complaining about. So I had a battle there. It was also a battle to get extra money but eventually we did. Here other parts of the structure were important. Children's officers were not top local authority officials. Once, when a family was getting evicted, I was getting nowhere with the housing manager. So I took the whole family and put them in his office and faced him with the fact that the children would have to go into care. I got support from the county clerk over this. The committee backed me in setting up a structure, including housing, to consider homelessness. The committee were sympathetic but moralistic. They were more interested in individual children than in strategies. There was a sub-committee to which you had to report regularly about every child and members participated actively.

One advantage in Scotland is that the Scots did not fight "residence." In Lancashire if you took a child into care from a place which was not his normal residence then you had to try to get his home authority to pay. Time, effort and money were spent on this. That did not happen in Scotland. Lennox Castle Hospital was in the bounds of Stirlingshire and a number of babies were born there and had to be taken into care. Nobody ever argued about it.

We had to start undertaking preventative work, raising standards in recruitment, improving residential care My impression was that my authority took children in almost on demand, children who could cope at home with support. Prevention did take off but in a different sense than usual. We did a lot of weekly collecting of rents to avoid evictions. It was the only way we could plug that hole of children coming needlessly into care. Gradually other departments — Health and Education — began to notice our prevention and came in with us. That was exciting. The children's committee did not oppose prevention but they had some reservations before they eventually supported it. We spent time on prevention and gradually they let us spend money. Once the treasurer was becoming quite agitated about parents who were in arrears over parental contributions for children who were in care. I asked him to accompany me on a Friday night when we went round to the families. He came and once he saw their plight he never pressed the matter again.

In Scotland, there was a good core of child care people. Bill McNeil, the children's officer for Renfrew was one. They were well equipped to contribute to the debate about reorganization. They had good relationships with voluntary bodies, especially adoption societies. But not with the courts. In Lancashire, the Children's Department had a formal role with the juvenile courts and even had to apply for affiliation orders. That never happened in Scotland.

In the 1960s, child care did improve in Scotland, partly because it began to get more trained staff, partly because the Children's Departments in the cities, Glasgow, Edinburgh, Dundee and Aberdeen, began to improve and they tended to set the pace. People like Vera Hiddlestone, who worked in Midlothian, Kay Carmichael and Megan Browne were a powerful force. Jimmy Johnston was another, highly regarded figure who moved from the civil service to be a director of a Social Work Department. Local government itself was beginning to change and became more outward looking. There was a churning of thought and a sense of hopefulness.

The Association of Child Care Officers did not initially have the same influence in Scotland as in England because it did not have so many members. But in the 1960s Scottish children's officers became more active in the Scottish Children's Officers Association (SCOA). Bill McNeil was the leading figure. Margaret Urquhart was heavily involved. She was the epitome of the personal children's officer, she, more than anybody, had direct relationships with children. She had a standing and quite a following. She was a comforting figure, tolerant, understanding and hopeful and you would never have guessed that she had been in the Metropolitan Police. Edward Thomas from Edinburgh was a senior member. I later became secretary. It forged links with the Scottish Office and liaised with the voluntary sector. It also had connections with Scandinavia and would invite speakers from there to its conferences. This was probably where the ideas for children's panels came from.

By the time I came to Scotland, reorganization was in the air. SCOA pushed the interests of social work. It included a number of members who had come up from poor law and welfare departments. Some of these held back from the Kilbrandon proposals but the body of the kirk pushed for them. We had to fight probation who were totally opposed. Some of the voluntary children's societies were also very defensive and fought a rear guard action against change. But there were exceptions, progressive people in voluntary bodies like Janet Lusk and Julie Ann McQueen of the Scottish Council for Unmarried Mothers. Personally, I wanted child care services to be surrounded by other services so that children in families could be better supported. I wanted the other departments to be incorporated. Kilbrandon also brought in the concept of children's panels. Interestingly, I recall Kilbrandon giving a talk and saying that panels could be applied to adults as well as children. The Children's Departments got involved in the training of panel members in anticipation of their inauguration.

In retrospect, I felt we had achieved something in the Children's Department at Stirlingshire I remember someone saying that they now saw newspaper adverts to recruit foster parents and using particular children's situations — which had never happened before. We moved forward, achieved better standards, got children back home earlier, met children's needs more appropriately, residential staff were given better support.

I became director of social work in Argyll. I have no qualification in saying that the creation of Social Work Departments was right. We made mistakes. The concept that any social worker can work with any client was wrong. Child care did lose out on that. Initially there was bureaucratic confusion plus disgruntled former probation officers. But change was essential to get the structure and framework for families. Previously there had been fifty-two different Children's Departments and the range of practice was enormous from the acceptable to the grossly intolerable. Some could not afford either material of human resources. So rationalization into bigger units had to bring benefits. Further the Children's Hearings did involve more lay people in the system, often people who understood the issues — although I worried that so many teachers became members. The Children's Hearings do provide justice as well as welfare for children. Also at this time the approved schools became List D schools and merged into the general range of provision and benefited from the environment of social work.

Following the reorganization of local authority boundaries, I became divisional director of social services in Lanarkshire in 1975. I supported the move to larger authorities. For instance, Argyll found huge advantages from going into Strathclyde Region and not only for social work. It meant that it had a capital infrastructure for bridges and harbours which it could not do on its own. Social work gained access to training and support. It meant that services could be spread much more evenly over a large area.

I reluctantly retired in 1986 when I was sixty. Looking around today, I get worried about the loss of public support for social work and the barrage of constant criticism. I worry that young people will not want to become social workers as a career. Social work is grimly hanging on rather than becoming a force for development in society and a source of satisfaction for the recipients and the social workers.

Brian Roycroft

Introduction
Brian Roycroft was born in Frodsham, Cheshire. His parents were houseparents with the National Children's Homes so his childhood was spent in various residential establishments. After training at Leeds and Birmingham Universities, he became a child care officer in Hertfordshire in 1957. From 1961-1964 he was an assistant area officer in the children's department of the LCC. From 1964-1967 he served as children's officer for Gateshead and then for Newcastle-Upon-Tyne from 1967-1971. He was director of the Newcastle Social Services Department from 1971-1993. Since his retirement, Brian has been active in national and local voluntary agencies and is chairperson of the Alzheimer's Disease Society.

Interview
I started my first job as a children's officer at Gateshead in 1964. I was nearly thirty-one years of age and the town clerk sent me out to buy a bowler hat and informed me this was to be worn attending council meetings. The council and committees were very structured. Chief officers presented reports but only spoke when invited. I learnt to exert control before meetings and to rehearse certain councillors on their lines in advance. I learnt my place in the pecking order. At council meetings, the chief officers sat from the town clerk and chief constable downwards. I sat nearly at the bottom, one above the baths superintendent.

The department had three children's homes, six child care officers and four administrative staff. I was the only one who had a car allowance and the only one with any sort of training. In the three children's homes, there were a total of sixteen staff. I was quickly aware that six of these were totally unsuitable. One home, Brierdene, with thirty-five children, had a rotten old building, large dormitories, the food was execrable, the clothing of Poor Law standards and visiting hours for relatives strictly limited. One home was a decent family group home. The third home posed as a hostel for girls but was more like the town brothel. The department had 205 children in care. Thirty-five were in foster care, sixty-two in our own residential homes, the rest in voluntary homes or approved schools all over the UK. Once in care few children were rehabilitated unless the original cause of admission was simple such as illness of the mother. A sub-committee approved foster parents and the placements of children. The advice of the town clerk's wife was sought for she was a trained nurse!

After assessing the situation, I laid down my objectives. They were to close two of the children's homes and get rid of unsuitable staff, to get training for the child care officers; to bring the distant children back to Gateshead; to increase boarding-out; to get better pay and conditions for staff. In this I got strong support from the Home Office inspectors and from the chairman of the children's committee, Joe Roberts. Joe was partially deaf and blind following accidents in the mines. He was a man of absolute integrity, an old fashioned socialist who believed firmly in the welfare state. Five foot one inch tall and a girth of similar measurements, a prodigious capacity for beer, this man was a tower of strength.

With Joe's support, I recruited two child care officers straight from courses. The council, after a full debate, agreed to second one officer a year for training. Closing the children's homes was a more difficult matter. Eventually the Home Office child care inspectorate came to my aid in the form of Val Scerri. He produced in confidence a damning report for me which got leaked to the *Gateshead Post*. My subsequent report to the full council rebutting the allegations was so weak as to induce the wrath of many and the closure of Brierdene. I was learning the devious ways of successful politics!

I sacked the staff from the girl's hostel and replaced them by the excellent couple, Mr and Mrs Kathy Craig, from the family group home where I appointed another good couple. All of these changes could only be achieved by increasing foster care and making user agreements with neighbouring authorities and voluntary organizations.

While at Gateshead I became very aware of child abuse within families. As a child care officer, I had met physical abuse. I knew little about sexual abuse, although no doubt it was going on. There was beating of children, burning them with cigarettes. Usually the NSPCC were called in and they then asked the Children's Department to take the children into care. In Gateshead we had two very good child care officers, both untrained, who were very good at detecting physical abuse and then perceived sexual abuse. We took one case of sexual abuse to court where we prosecuted — which was unusual — and I remember being taken aside by the chairman of the magistrates who said it was not nice for the community to have these kinds of things identified; he felt I should have dealt with it in a more low key manner.

At Gateshead, I also became concerned about what was happening to some of the children in the larger homes. The staff had been appointed by the councillors and they included a couple of men I was certain were fiddling with the boys and girls. I interviewed some of the children and got nowhere. But I did sack them. I made mistakes — I appointed someone who did abuse children. Today there is a danger that we become too obsessed with sexual abuse and so ignore other forms, such as neglect and indifference, which can be equally damaging.

The child care officers were wonderful people, eager to learn and tireless workers. We enjoyed teach-in sessions two evenings every week. Theory was discussed and cases examined and they began to produce high quality work. After three years, the Gateshead Children's Department was regarded in the profession as "a little gem." These words were used by the regional head of child care inspectors, Mr Joseph, at a conference in Durham in 1966. My staff and committee burst with pride and my children's officer colleagues were amazingly tolerant.

I must comment on the children's officers. When I started as a young child care officer, I came across this strange anachronism created by the second world war. Many had lost their boy friends or husbands in the war. They were very intelligent and today would be heads of big business or chief executives in local authorities. At that time there were very few jobs for women of this kind, perhaps a matron in a hospital. The only top job they could get in local government was children's officer. They were tremendously strong characters. They had such a clear vision as to where they wanted child care to go. This was a shared experience because they talked with each other in the Association of Children's Officers. They were formidable in their education, their energy, and their presence. Barbara Kahan, Lucy Faithfull, Gwynneth Wansborough-Jones, Beti Jones, Priscilla Young, Margery Taylor, the incomparable Lady Amicia Carroll and the glamorous Sylvia Watson. When I joined Hertfordshire, Sylvia Watson was the children's officer and, with her assistant, John Stroud, encouraged young officers to do unorthodox things which were in the interest of children. During the 1960s, more men came to prominence such as Tom White, Bill Freeman and Bob Bessell who implemented further changes. I got great support from the Association of Children's Officers.

When the post of children's officer at Newcastle fell vacant, one of their powerful councillors, Teresa Russell, invited me to apply. There were three candidates and, as I waited for my turn, a porter called me to the telephone. The phone was in a small booth and I was shocked to find Mrs Russell crouched on the floor. "Be careful of the catholics," she hissed. A few minutes later I was summoned to the committee room and as I entered Teresa Russell and the chairman, Mary Shaw, rose from their chairs and kissed me. I had a feeling that the job was mine.

In 1967, the state of the Newcastle Children's Department was worse than that of that of Gateshead in 1963. In fairness, there were twelve family group homes and an excellent reception centre. But no staff were trained. All applications for children to be admitted to care were interviewed by an admissions officer who ascertained whether it fell within the criteria of the 1948 Children Act. If it fitted, he sent a child care officer to admit the child. Each family group home was staffed by a married couple with a living-in assistant. The man followed his own trade. It was fraught with problems. Firstly, a lack of training. Secondly, burn-out through exhaustion. Thirdly, the men kept running away with the young assistants. The reception home, Ferwood was in a fine building. Food and physical standards were excellent but child care practices were abominable. Later when I recruited Steve Casson, it and other homes offered more sensitive care.

By vigorous public relations and wooing students at training courses. I attracted staff and after four years the proportion of qualified reached nearly 60 per cent. I made friends with William Utting who had been the chief probation officer before becoming a lecturer at the university. He helped me greatly in my recruitment drive and I invited him to work within the department raising social work standards. He went on to other things.

My interest in prevention had started as a child care officer in Hertfordshire. I was hauled up before the chief clerk because I had submitted a claim to travel to see some families without considering that they were to enter care. Eventually I was told it was okay to claim for preventative work. Sylvia Watson must have intervened. Then she took me to lunch and quizzed me about what I was doing with the families. I think it was part of a small survey she was doing and she became one of the driving forces for prevention. The Children and Young Persons Act (1963) then legitimized what we were doing. But, in some ways, its implementation both in Gateshead and Newcastle was farcial. When I arrived in Newcastle there were 580 children in care but by 1971 it was over a 1,000. The Act enabled departments to obtain more staff so that in Newcastle I was able to get the numbers of child care officers increased from fifteen to twenty so as to implement the new duties. The officers then identified more need so more came into care. It also moved more children out of care because it allowed staff to do the preparation to get them home. The length of time children spent in care dropped dramatically and this changed the nature of residential and foster care — including greater use of relatives as foster parents.

Until I became a children's officer, I did not appreciate that approved schools were like castles in the countryside where they were the biggest employer and biggest purchaser of supplies. I recall discussing with managers whether corporal punishment should be abolished. A wealthy lady manager, declared "I would never dream of training a horse without a whip and boys should be trained in the same spirit." When I suggested that one school took girls as well as boys, the headmaster protested that he might not have enough boys for the cricket team. These heads and managers had almost complete control and were deciding when children were discharged yet it was a lottery whether they went there or into care in the first place.

Many of the schools tried to give a quality of life by the traditional means of sport, good food and training for certain jobs. Yet the youngsters were isolated from their parents while their vocational training as farm workers or sailors — was becoming irrelevant. The White Paper *Children in Trouble* was one of the most sensible ever produced. Barbara Kahan took the proposals forward. The approved school heads considered her the devil incarnate but she was my heroine because she proclaimed that many approved schools damaged children. Probably the Association of Child Care Officers did even more than the Association of Children's Officers to shape the Children and Young Persons Act (1969). ACCO could be more political than ACO and it won the ear of David Ennals and Barbara Castle in the Labour Party. The act was a success in so far as it was implemented. At least it made clear that local authorities were in charge of the former approved schools. I was able to insist on changes on the three in my area so that they were more geared to children's needs.

I was enthusiastic about the Seebohm Report and the ensuing legislation allowed local authorities to set up a different social services structure. When I started as director there was excitement and resources. The last years were dreadful, closing homes, cutting budgets, mentally I could not go on with that. Today I feel dreadfully sorry for the people in social work. I would take out the purchaser/provider divide. I would make social workers responsible for the care of individuals all the way through. And I would make social services committees much more responsible for them. Members of children's committees visited the places where children in care were placed and so they were much more knowledgeable when decisions were made. Now they are told, "We have contracts for seventy old people's homes" and they do not know the individual situations. I would press for a return to the position when committees are not just accountable but are responsible for all aspects of a person's care.

The tragedies have made child protection the high profile area of child care. The counterpart is that many of the skills in fostering and residential care have been lost in the anxiety to ensure it is a properly protected service. It is hard now for social workers to take risks. I took awful risks some of which had disastrous outcomes but others moved things forward. Similarly, the national child care voluntary bodies have lost their campaigning zeal because they have become the tools of the statutory services and so find it difficult to have a separate identity.

Within the Children's Departments, staff were more involved with children despite high caseloads. They knew the children better than social workers today. I still have contact with children who were in my care in Gateshead Take after-care, child care officers had no structure to maintain the after-care of children but many did so because you had known the children for a long time and were fond of them. There was a freedom to do so. In retirement, I have become involved with three local voluntary bodies, including a children's adventure group, and it is strange that I have returned to what it was like before, I am close enough to all the staff to know what is going on and to know the customers.

Val Scerri

Introduction

Valentino John Scerri was born in 1933. His mother died when he was two and his father, who was in the British army, placed Val in a convent home in Jerusalem. Aged twelve, he was moved to the UK to live with an uncle. He took a maths degree at Leicester University and, while there, had to spend nine months in hospital with TB. The time for reflection caused him to decide he wanted to do social work. He undertook the social studies certificate at Leicester University in 1959 and then the child care course at Birmingham University. His first child care post was with the Worcester City Children's Department. After a spell doing medical social work with the Leicester City Health Department and a short stay with Birmingham Children's Department, he went to the Nottinghamshire Children's Department as a child care officer and was promoted to area children's officer. In 1968, Val joined the Home Office child care inspectorate. He was appointed director of Salford Social Services Department in 1970 and remained there until his retirement in 1992.

Interview

After qualifying, my first post was with Worcester City Children's Department at a salary of £450. The field staff consisted of Miss Ida Davies, the children's officer, and myself. She did the girls and I did the boys and now I covered the full range of work. Worcester had a 100 kids in care so it was a tremendous learning experience. The week after I started, Miss Davies announced that, as she had not had any leave for a year, she was going away for a week, and that I would have to take the children's committee. Today social workers would not see the main committee for 10-20 years.

There was a cottage homes which had three cottages, fifteen children in each, boys, girls and mixed infants. My job was to board-out the children and eventually close it. I did it. The matron was a formidable lady. I remember taking a girl in and the matron said to me, "Mr Scerri, that girl has a used look." It has always stayed with me because it so precisely summed her up. Years later, when I was in Nottinghamshire, that girl turned up at Rampton Mental Hospital where she was a patient and having a baby and I arranged the adoption.

After three years in Worcester, I did a spell at Leicester City Health Department doing TB work. Health social work followed by a short period with Birmingham Children's Department. Then I went to Nottinghamshire as a child care officer. The children's officer was Rosalie Treece who was a superb administrator and who fought to get improvements through committee. It was tremendous contrast with Worcester for now I had a structure and an organization. But child care officers still had a great deal of independence. I just did not like children and young people being in care so I would do anything to keep them out. I would prop up difficult circumstances and every year a child grew older I would think, "Well, at least he is still with his mum and dad." I considered myself good with problem families and once I was being accompanied by a Home Office inspector; I took her to this dim mother in a filthy home to display the marvellous relationship I had made; she had a fat stomach and I asked her when the baby was due; the inspector gave me a funny look and then I saw a drawer on the floor with the new baby in it. The woman hadn't changed shape.

Child abuse is more public now. As a child care officer I think if I had dug deeper I might have found more of it. I believed strongly in preserving family and love and perhaps subconsciously I did not follow up any suspicions. Later I recall an abusing father was convicted of abusing his daughter; an older daughter, by then married, came and told me he had done it to her but that he had been a wonderful father and she loved him very much. It made me think. Was I right not to follow up my suspicions and so keep the family together?

After a while, I was promoted to area children's officer at Worksop. I was also active in the Association of Child Care Officers (ACCO). It was a small body of people but we had much in common. The annual conference was highly regarded. As a student at Birmingham, Pauline Shapiro almost forced us to go. As a new child care officer in Worcester I found myself elected treasurer for the regional branch. In Worcester I was the only child care officer and ACCO's regional meetings gave me colleagues who were really supportive. It gave me contacts with other Children's Departments whom I could phone for advice. ACCO also had a tremendous relationship with the Home Office and co-operated in policy making. It had a number of fine presidents, Tom White and Janie Thomas in particular. The annual conferences were especially important. I recall going to Swanwick for them and the officers all arriving in small cars, Ford Poplars and Morris Minors. It was a very supportive organization and it meant that you got to know other child care officers in other departments by name. I was on ACCO's committee when the conference was moved to Nottingham and then to Manchester where over a 1,000 attended. The conferences were very serious and for years we did not talk about salaries; the professional content was very high with people talking about fostering, adoption and prevention.

In 1966, by which time Joan Cooper was Chief Inspector at the Home Office Children's Department, I was appointed an inspector at the age of thirty-three. Having been a child care officer, I knew all the dodges when you were inspected. I once inspected Brian Roycroft's department in Newcastle. I looked at some case files and noticed that all the recent reports were in the same writing in the same ink. Brian had to admit that they had all been written up the night before. But Joan encouraged her staff to think and not just carry out mechanical inspections.

As an inspector, I saw the contrast between departments. I had come from a very good one in Nottinghamshire. But some were appalling. One of the worst was a large authority; when I went there the children's officer was still doing all the *Guardian ad Litem* cases. You could not see him for files. In 1968, it still had cottage homes, six cottages with 10 kids in each and the officer in charge also had responsibility for a large old people's home. The staff had little idea.

The Home Office was basically a controlling ministry, responsible for prisons, police, immigration, so it was pleased to have a positive department like children's. The Home Office was a senior ministry and carried a lot of clout. So it was possible to have some influence. Often you helped at the request of children's officers and attended committees because they asked you. Many Children's Departments were very small and the children's officers needed help. If an inspector was getting nowhere with a children's officer, he would see the chairman who might then involve the town clerk who, in those days, had a lot of power. As an inspector, you did not write letters; you sent in reports and civil servants composed letters which were signed at a senior level. I remember visiting a detention centre run by the police. In my report I mentioned that the decor was a dreadful green, awful if parents were visiting. Because it was in the report, it got changed. Home Office inspectors had authority. Personally, I had a philosophy about child care and I pushed it — namely that a child was an individual and systems came second to children's needs.

The Home Office favoured fostering. Perhaps it was pushed too far by some departments for the view became that second rate fostering was better than no fostering. We overlooked the failures, the children who were moved around a lot and suffered as a result. I don't think many fosterings became that permanent. After leaving care at 18, many children drifted back to their own parents. But the pressure was necessary. It got the big institutions closed. And not just the Children's Departments. I recall co-operating with Father Gauguan, a wonderful man, of the Catholic Rescue Society in Newcastle who set up family group homes and fostering.

One of the important sides of the Home Office was its training programme which was exceptional. It meant that departments like Nottinghamshire were annually sending 10-20 staff on courses funded by the Central Council for Training in Child Care. Joan Cooper made us more than inspectors. She added the professional child care side. She was able to talk about quality and the niceties of child care.

The Children's Departments represented that deprived children required a special system of care and that artificial parenting, like fostering, required special efforts. It was the Children's Departments which achieved the professionalization of social work. Partly this was because the Home Office, with its emphasis on training, made for a strong difference between Children's and Welfare Departments.

The Curtis Report and the 1948 Children Act spoke about children's officers as women. They brought a female influence into local government which had been dominated by men. They brought in a parental influence. The chief welfare officers, who had often been around a long time, were men, administrators. Some were caring individuals but they did not have the fervour and fire which the women children's officers introduced. They were the kind of people who, if the children's committee would not agree to something, would sometimes pay for it out of their own pockets. It was not just a job to them which is something which has been lost today. I have mentioned Rosalie Treece as a fine children's officer. She frightened some people and, if she did not think much of you, she could wipe the floor with you. There were others, Margaret Brooke-Willis at Cheshire, Sylvia Watson at Hertfordshire, Kathleen Ruddock at Leicestershire. They were very similar in type, mostly middle-class, often having done evacuation work in the war, none of them trained. I am sure that if the existing welfare officers had got their jobs, it would not have been the same.

The new service also produced child care officers who believed in themselves and were prepared to act. Today social workers can not do anything without asking permission or going to a case conference. I had a hundred children in care yet I never felt over-worked and I was never behind. I did not have to spend much time in discussions.

The Seebohm changes had to happen because the differentiation between children's and adult services was inappropriate. It was also about status and money unfortunately. The salaries of directors of social services put them on a par with other local government chief officers such as directors of education. It meant you were able to get involved in social policy and social planning which is the real prevention. For the first five years of the new departments there was an obsession with integration and child care took a terrible wallop. The child care philosophy is about parenting and this could not easily be integrated into welfare philosophy. Child care had been the best resourced and had the highest professional quality so it had to be watered down as other services came up. Social workers had to become generic, they could not stay in child care. After five years or so Social Services Departments introduced children's sections. But good things were lost.

Today there is still good and bad child care. But now it can occur within departments because they are so large that standards differ between areas. One matter has been disastrous from the point of view of professional standards. The purchaser/provider split in which part of the service buys from another shows that it is now just about money. That upsets me and makes me angry.

Margery Taylor

Introduction

Born in 1920, Margery Taylor was brought up in Felstead, Essex by her father, an industrial chemist, and a caring and intellectual mother. On leaving school, she worked as a secretary for a firm of window manufacturers and persuaded them to transfer her to London once the war started. From 1945-1948, she studied social science at the London School of Economics and then undertook the child care course where she was taught by Clare Britton and Donald Winnicott. She then joined the Nottinghamshire Children's Department. In 1955, she became deputy children's officer in Kent and was simultaneously the children's officer of Canterbury. From 1959-1965, she was chief inspector in child care with the Children's Department of the London County Council. From 1965-1974, she served as the director of training with the London Boroughs Training Committee. She became director of social services with Redbridge in 1974 until her retirement in 1983.

Interview

Leaving LSE, I went to Nottinghamshire as a child care officer based at the area office in Worksop. It was a mining area so I thought the first thing I should do was to go down a mine. That was an education and I realized a little of what life was like underground. It was a very tight-knit community, strong families, very chauvinistic, with wives talking about their husbands as "masta" and not knowing how much they earned. Also in Nottinghamshire was Rampton and I remember my first visit, feeling very apprehensive as I walked across the exercise ground with these odd and frightening looking men — and I a young and inexperienced social worker. This started my interest in mental health.

Within the Children's Department there was a lot of excitement and a feeling that if we got it right we could make life better for a whole range of children and young people. There were lots of old fashioned children's homes, cottage homes, yet they often contained housemothers who may not have had a great deal of imagination, but who provided real care and continuity. They taught me that it was all very well coming in with our new ideas but we had to build on what was there. The children officer was Rosalie Spence (later Treece), a very strong-minded person. You had to be prepared to argue your point and, if you did, she accepted you and encouraged you. She fought like anything for resources for the department and obtained them.

When I became deputy children's officer after a couple of years, I found we had to work very hard at making relationships with other departments. Rosalie Spence had been very successful in building up the Children's Department sometimes at the expense of other departments. I found I was able to make bridges with education, probation, and the police. As deputy children's officer, I did much of the court work. In working with other departments, you mainly related with men yet I never found that matters got polarized. I always thought of myself as working in a particular setting with a job to do, sometimes you worked with men, sometimes with women, but they were all colleagues. Gender never became an issue.

Nottinghamshire Children's Department was prepared to experiment and the staff really cared. There was a feeling of bringing houseparents and foster parents into the team. It did achieve the recognition that the children and the families with whom we were working were just as important as and should have the same opportunities as children living with their own parents. We were working to keep families together well before the Children and Young Persons Act (1963).

There was child abuse. A few horrific cruelty cases. Some child neglect. I remember two very mentally handicapped parents living in a council house with eight children. The first time I went in, they were sitting around a table with chicken wire around the bottom part with a slot in it to feed the chickens. The NSPCC obtained a court order to remove the children. The family barricaded themselves in — for there was a fierce love for the children — and said they would only let the children go if I came. So I removed them. I still do not know if that was right. The parents were unconventional and did not keep the usual standards but the love was there. They kept in touch with the children and, when the children left care the first thing they did was to go home. The look of joy on their faces was memorable.

I recall, in a remote part, a difficult case of incest. There were two to three farm cottages with the families interrelated and everybody slept with everybody else. It was a pattern of life. The children were very bewildered when they were removed. Today things are much more black and white in child protection yet I do not think human beings are like that. You need to find out what does the most damage to children and how you should handle the situation. I am not saying that the sexual abuse of children is right. I am saying that where it happens you have to be very careful indeed about how you handle it and not make it worse by too harsh attitudes.

I left Nottinghamshire in 1955 and went to Kent, where 2000 children were in care, as deputy to Elizabeth Harvie. Simultaneously I was children's officer of the small city of Canterbury. Elizabeth was not a trained social worker, was very intelligent, great sense of humour, marvellous sense of what people really needed. Irritating to work with sometimes because she was not the best organizer but she had vision and knew what she wanted to achieve. She kept in touch with dozens of children once they moved out of care. She took no notice of those tiresome people in the Treasurer's Department. She worked very well with education and health. Her vision was to restore children who had a rough time, to help them mend their families, and to help them stand on their own feet and operate in the community. I saw her recently just before she died and she was full of faith and hope.

Within Kent, I had primary responsibility for the area offices and for the case conferences at the two reception centres. Fostering was well developed and we began drawing foster parents together. But we were not obsessed with getting a high position in the boarding-out league. We wanted the most appropriate placement for the children. A lot depended on the quality of staff. Fortunately we did obtain a high proportion of qualified child care officers. Residential staff quality was more varied. When it was good it was very good, when it was bad it was horrid. We recruited some trained residential staff but not many. They did work under tremendous pressures and we tried to build support systems with other professionals like teachers and psychiatrists.

I recall a mother removing her three-year-old child from a cottage home. She was unstable and had ill-treated the child so we had to get her back. She was living in a caravan across two fields. I was deputed to go. The mother was pretty disturbed but we talked and finally she said, "If you leave the child, I'll hand her over in the morning. If you bring the police, I'll kill her." I took three deep breaths and said, "Alright, we've got a contract." I didn't sleep a wink that night, went back in the morning and the child was handed over to me. I was terrified but I was using judgement.

ACCO was important to me. It was necessary in order to learn from and to support each other. It meant that the things we were doing could be brought together and so be a force in influencing policy. I became president and went all over the country. ACCO did have some influence on government and its journal *ACCORD*, edited by John Stroud, had some impact.

I left Kent in 1959 and went as chief inspector in child care with the Children's Department of the London County Council. It had a knowledgeable children's committee, with members like Bee Serota and Peggy Jay, a good team of inspectors including Kenneth Urwin, and good support from the Education and Welfare Departments. It was a sad day when the LCC was abolished in 1965.

I became director of training with the London Boroughs Training Committee. The thread that has run through the whole of my professional life is an awareness of the importance of training. People need opportunities to examine what they have learned from their practice in company with those who have got other kinds of experience and knowledge. They are then able to formulate and articulate it more effectively. We had training days for councillors and courses that brought residential and field staff together. We started training for management.

I took part in the lobbying for the implementation of the Seebohm Report. I still think Seebohm was right and that the separation of mental, health, welfare and children's services was wrong. In 1974 I became director of the Redbridge Social Services Department and retired in 1983.

Social workers today don't know what they are supposed to be doing and they don't know what casework is. Social work should be an understanding of what goes on inside people and what goes on outside them in social institutions and how the two interact. Today some social workers think that all they are about is implementing the law and some think it is just about practical things. They face a bad press, political correctness, and the purchaser/provider split. I feel very sad because, at its best, social work can contribute so much to overcoming human difficulties.

The great contribution of the Children's Departments was to add to the understanding of what went on in families. They showed that not all things which appear bad in families are necessarily destructive to the persons to whom it is happening. The departments made a number of people realize how much they had to give — through fostering, for example — and how much their own lives could be enriched. Children's officers were often formidable people like Gwyneth Wansborough-Jones, Sylvia Watson, Beryl Watson, Dorothy Watkins, Barbara Kahan, Ted Brown and Beti Jones. They believed in action, so different from the grey directors of today with their convoluted words. We wanted to be a part of it with them and got on with the job.

In spite of all the difficulties, I most remember the sense of fulfilment. We made mistakes but we were doing something worthwhile. I remember one man coming to see me; he was about to get married and wanted to know more about his family. I became aware of the importance of being available and so giving people the bits that are important. I felt aware of what a valuable thing we were doing.

Rosalie Treece (formerly Spence)

Introduction
After the early death of her father, Rosalie Spence went to a boarding school at the age of nine. She disliked it and believes that this early experience contributed to her strong belief that children should be with their own parents. During the war, she studied social science at LSE and then went as a welfare officer and assistant billeting officer to a district in Northamptonshire where she was responsible for fifty-two villages. She later worked for the Central Council for Information. After the war, she was a county welfare officer in Devon where she looked after boarded-out children and residual evacuees. From 1948-1971, she was children's officer for Nottinghamshire County Council.

Interview
I started at Nottinghamshire on 1 July, 1948. It was a new department and we were taking over responsibilities from people who were very long established. The medical officer of health, the director of education and the public assistance people didn't want to give up any of their responsibilities, particularly to a woman chief officer. I was thirty-four, very young. The men used to say you can get anything you like because you are a woman but it wasn't like that. They would also say women don't know anything about this sort of thing. This made me aggressive, I wouldn't give way. I had a few

tussles with the treasury and they always wanted to keep the brakes on. And certain procedures I had to get them to relax. We had to pass our requisitions on to the treasury and they would ask questions like, "Why are you ordering chicken so often?" We had a residential nursery where the washing was done nearby at what had been a Public Assistance institution. The nappies came back stiff and not white and the matron wanted them sent to a private laundry. The officials in the treasury were opposed to the cost of this so I took a pile of the nappies to the finance committee and we got our way.

To start with I only had three or four child care officers, then I had seven. It kept expanding. Then we had five area offices with area children's officers. The biggest step forward was having male officers in the earliest stages. Everyone thought I was a bit crazy when I said we wanted men but we got them.

One of the difficulties was combining the administrative and social work sides for I was first and foremost interested in the children, a social worker. I had a good man as chief clerk and later deputy. He was good at getting out the reports and on the administrative side. I organized the department into four sections, the investigative section which dealt with court work — under a very good man who knew the law — care, that is children in care, residential establishments, and administration.

I had to work very long hours because I attended nearly all the committee meetings and I also wanted to get out to be with the children. I visited the children's homes and I felt it important to support all the staff, including the domestic staff, and I knew their circumstances. I knew the children and when a child was eighteen and left care I would see them and go through their file with them.

We had a group of seven cottage homes which I gradually replaced by smaller homes. We had several smaller homes for about 14-16 children. We obtained a hostel for girls and one for boys who were going out to work. We had two residential nurseries. One was attached to the cottage homes and I closed that. The other residential nursery had been built just before the war and was full of babies. I very soon changed that and introduced the babies into the children's homes and just kept the very vulnerable babies there.

Staff morale was very good. I did a lot of fighting for them and got an extra weeks holiday for the child care staff in lieu of the extra long and unpaid hours they worked. It was hard to get good residential staff. I had no hesitation in sacking them if I thought they were not suitable. The children used to confide in me as well. I sacked one man for whacking the children with a poker. It was important to feel you could really trust the staff. To a certain extent we had trouble in recruiting residential staff but matters improved when we got a good reputation. We used to have sports days for the children to which we would invite members and staff from the treasury and architects sections and all the children from the homes would be there. It was great fun. Then the child care officers would take me to foster homes, for instance when someone had been a foster mother for a long time and I would thank them. And when children were confirmed I would present them with a prayer book. I knew all the children's circumstances and, when we had our case meetings once a month, the child care officer would answer any questions but I could always give a resume of why the child came into care — and we had 500 children.

It was long hours. When I started I was not married. I put my heart and soul into it. I never got in until eight at night. I had friends but not much time for them. There was a sense of mission, one of commitment. I wanted the children to get the best out of life. I had a great belief that the children's place was with their parents if at all possible. I was rather tough with some of the child care officers sometimes. I wouldn't let them bring some children into care. I remember a young child care officer wanted a very young baby to come into care and I said no. About a day after I made this decision, the baby was smothered in its parents bed. So I got the child care officer to come in and said, "You were not to blame in any way. I made the decision. Don't blame yourself." There was another case where we had a very good child care officer, doing pioneer work with families, and a father threatened he would commit suicide unless she took the children into care. "Here's the key of the house, I'm throwing myself off the bridge," he said and went off. But she stood firm.

The children's committee was very good. I had four chairmen and the one who did the most was Alderman Mrs Sharrard. The members were not really policy makers but they took tremendous interest. There was a rota for visiting the children's homes, the approved schools, and the hostels, two members at a time. They saw the staff and children on their own. But they did not interfere with any of the children's arrangements, although they would report to me if they thought anything should be done. They were supportive.

Nottinghamshire did have a good reputation for fostering before I went there — built up by the assistant director of education, Mr Revell. We increased it and got up to over 70 per cent. We were always recruiting foster parents. In those days we did not foster the very difficult children. We did foster babies with a view to adoption. It is difficult to put adolescent children in foster homes unless there was some connection with the home already. We tended to use the hostels for them.

We were busy, doing all things all the time. I remember my deputy saying. "I wish we could consolidate for a bit." But I was anxious to do preventive work with families. I had certain funds from charities which I could use — before 1963. We used to take mothers and children away on holidays. I did a lot of talking with the committee about how much cheaper prevention was. We had co-ordinating committees with police, housing people, medical officers of health, clerks of the justices. I used to organize that. First, we had public meetings and talked with local people about the need for co-ordination. Then we had case conferences at a local level on certain families. The greatest problem was housing. We used to work with families in Part 3 Accommodation and getting them rehoused was a very uphill struggle. Of course, unemployment wasn't such a problem then. All the child care officers were keen on preventative work and in each area we would have one who specialized in it.

A good child care officer was one who could relate to all sorts and conditions but at the same time not get personally involved. They had to size up a situation and press for what was really necessary and bring in help and advice from other sources. We had an excellent staff, all qualified people. Margaret Evans and Val Scerri who both went to the Home Office, Ted Brown, who became a children's officer, Pat Thornton and Muriel Beaney, were all outstanding. They were feeding each other all the time, mixing together at case conferences and staff meetings so that we thought out policies together. Life at the top could be a bit isolated so I appreciated these colleagues. I also appreciated the Home Office inspectors who made a great contribution because they insisted on high child care standards.

I was secretary of the Midland Approved Schools Managers' Association and tried to change the approved schools. I was only too pleased when they finished. We had case conferences at the approved schools and reviewed the boys' progress. The headmasters did see themselves as tin gods. But I became very friendly with the head of Risley Hall and still see him.

The strength of the Children's Department was the commitment of the staff. They built up relationships with the children in care who had confidence in them so that complaints and worries could be aired. The department was small enough to be able to develop sound communications between staff through regular meetings of (a) child care officers and (b) area children's officers and (c) heads of establishments. We also had six monthly conferences for a proportion of all staff. Field, residential and administrative staff took children away on holidays. All this built up team spirit and made us feel part of an important concern. Our ultimate 'get together' was a residential three days with children about to leave care and an equal number of staff where everybody 'let their hair down' and the children told us what they thought about being in care.

In 1948, children in care were isolated or even worse, they were regarded as inferior beings. The Children's Departments gave respect and help to those who had to remain in care and we were able to restore so many more to their own families, which I am sure is the answer for it is only the exceptionable child who should be brought up away from his family — and if a very young child should be adopted.

I had a nice letter from one of my girls in care who has always kept in touch. She was a pain in the neck but has turned out alright and has trained as a nursery nurse.

She wrote this in a letter in 1995, "I think it is really nice that we have kept in touch. I have a great deal to thank you for, I am only where I am today because of you. You supported me and, most important of all, you believed in me. It was through you I did the Home Office course (NNEB). I never stop telling people about you. You are a very special lady." Another boy, now 50, phones up every other month.

Leslie Turner

Introduction
Leslie Turner was born in 1915 in Forest Gate, London. After school, he worked in the Electricity Department of the East Ham County Borough Council. He qualified as a member of the Institute of Chartered Secretaries and Administrators (and later obtained an external diploma in social studies from London University). Being in a reserved occupation, he remained with East Ham during the war and in 1948 was appointed as administrative assistant in its new Children's Department. In 1953 he was promoted to deputy children's officer. From 1955-1959, he was children's officer for Dudley, from 1959-1966 for Wolverhampton, and from 1966-1971 for Staffordshire. He was deputy director of the Social Services Department in Staffordshire until his retirement.

Interview
When I joined East Ham Children's Department as an administrative assistant, the children's officer was Harry Mapstone, who had been in charge of educational welfare. Field staff consisted of two female boarding out-out officers so he used to take me on visits to foster homes, children's homes and approved schools. He was full of the Curtis Report, full of enthusiasm. I became involved in the supervision of some boys. After Harry Mapstone left, Norman Lonsdale became children's officer and subsequently I became his deputy.

In 1955 I moved to Dudley as children's officer. My first duty was to visit a home where a child had died in suspicious circumstances. Soon after I was threatened by a notorious knife-carrying ex-prisoner whose children had refused to see him. With only two child care officers and three clerical staff, I used to take a share of the field work. At the juvenile court we made good relationships with the magistrates, the officials, the police and the probation officers.

Dudley had three children's homes with about forty places in all. My predecessor had built up a group of good reliable foster parents. Prevention started early. We tried to prevent homelessness. One day, a family turned up at the office having been evicted from their council house. They had half a dozen children who would cost the earth to take into care. I got very cross and contacted the Housing Department but the housing manager insisted, "They won't pay their rent, they've got to go." At the next council meeting, the housing manager said he resented the children's officer telling him what he should do with his tenants. But it did have some effect because afterwards, in such cases, they would ask us to see if we could do anything. There was another woman, rehoused in poor property, who refused to pay her rent. So on the days she got her family allowance from the post office, I would go with her and get her to hand over the rent. It kept the family together. With the passing of the years, it was clear that whatever the quality of care provided by the Children's Department, the best use of resources was to prevent the child coming away from home in the first place. Increasing effort was put into providing food, rent and domestic help to keep the home going. I was able to make a sibling of working age a foster parent to the several younger children of the family, whose parents had been killed in an accident, thereby preserving the family unit. Members of the council seemed to approve of our efforts.

The opportunity came to go to Wolverhampton, a much larger borough, in 1959. Despite its size, I still managed to visit a few children. Also, and I did this wherever I was children's officer, I visited all the children's homes regularly. I did not just go in and out, I stayed some time and knew all the staff who could tell me all their problems — whether it be administration, wanting a new carpet, or personal problems. Just as important, I knew most of the children, although not the short-term ones. I took note of what the Curtis Report said, that the officer was to have a personal responsibility. This is something which has been completely lost in the SSDs.

The children's committee was more political than in Dudley. But they came up with the resources. The problems of race were starting and I realized that we had to treat black children and adults on the same footing as white people. We did not then regard it as important to find foster parents of the same race as a child who needed a home, largely because there were few settled black families who could take on this role. To have kept a child suitable for fostering in a children's home when white foster parents were available would have seemed to us as a form of discrimination of the worst kind. Sometimes parents came to England, leaving adolescent children with grandparents. If they became very difficult they might be sent here to join their parents. But the parents might not have adequate accommodation. As a result there was a sharp rise for a time in the number of black children in care.

Wolverhampton had children in cottage homes which had to be closed. It was a matter of national policy, although I must say that the cottage homes did provide a community and friendships. We developed family group homes. One was excellent, based in a council house. They were suited for sibling groups or for children for whom foster homes could not he found. The children seemed to be fairly contented but the family group concept was difficult to maintain due to two factors. I found that over a period of one or two years, the membership of the 'family' completely changed. Children came and went (rehabilitation with parents was becoming more common) and so did the staff. Also, with the introduction of better working conditions, came the fixing of working hours, and the mother figure was not always there when the children came home from school. From the earliest days of Children's Departments, it had been recognized that to receive a child into care should be the last resort. If this could not be avoided, then a foster home would normally be best for a child.

The great impetus of the 1948 Children Act and the enthusiasm of dedicated child care officers led to a large increase in the number of children boarded out. There was an unofficial league table showing the percentage of foster children placed by different authorities. A high percentage of 80 was achieved in some places, but by the 1960s it began to be realized that a more realistic figure was probably 60 per cent. There were many breakdowns in the intervening years, and some children experienced a whole series of disastrous placings. Increasing skills led to a more careful approach to boarding-out and selection of foster parents. In Wolverhampton, I tried out the payment of salaries to a couple who then undertook to open their home to sibling groups, with the payment of the usual boarding-out allowances it was cheaper and more home-like. However, when the children returned to their parents the salary or retainer had to be continued, in order to have the home ready for use at possible short notice.

I was in Wolverhampton for seven years. We improved the residential side, gave people more defined roles, and gave the department a broader base by moving into areas. The average case load for the child care officers was down to forty.

I went to Staffordshire County Council in 1966. There were practically no area offices and the children's committee agreed to the setting up of offices in every town with a population of 20,000 or more. They made a base for the child care officers' work, cut down on travelling, made for easier liaison with residential staff, and they could be visited by clients. There was talk at the time of family advice centres, "the one door on which to knock", and we opened one in Brownfields, a part of Aldridge.

One difficulty was a children's home in Dawlish, Devon which was owned by the Staffordshire council. The idea was to send unhealthy children there where they went to local schools and were brought back to homes in Staffordshire at the end of term. It was a beautiful house, like a hotel with excellent food. I liked it but I didn't like the principle behind it. When the children came back they then had to be fitted into other residential establishments and this made the job of keeping siblings together all the harder. I considered the Dawlish home an unnecessary expense so we closed it.

One of the weaknesses of the child care services in 1948 had been the inadequacy of provision for the older boy or girl still in care at the age of eighteen. In the years that followed, local authorities were allowed to incur expenditure to assist in paying for lodgings, hostel accommodation and training. But resources were insufficient to provide adequate after care for many youngsters. We were helped by voluntary organizations who did good work in providing hostels. At one time residential training establishments, which bore some resemblance to approved schools (but without the stigma) were regarded as a godsend. One such was Turner's Court (Wallingford Farm Training School) but the demand for the less skilled farm worker was diminishing. For girls there was an even more limited choice. Some were happy to live at YWCA hostels. Again there was a great reliance upon the voluntary sector although we did have a working girls' hostel in Staffordshire.

Child abuse seems to have grown in recent years. I remember having quite a number of cases of ill-treatment and neglect but none so horrifying as more recent cases. In one case of sexual abuse of his daughters by a father (unknown to the mother) resulted in his being sent to prison. When he returned home, the magistrate's clerk suggested we should apply for an order to move the girls. For them it would seem that they were being punished. We decided that rehabilitation of the family with the support of the probation officer and a now vigilant mother was the best course. The girls felt no longer threatened by their father. After a long period of close supervision by the child care officer, it was apparent that the girls were no longer at risk.

I gave instructions to all my staff that any cases of neglect, ill-treatment, abuse, were to be put on my desk. In every case I had to know. Today, it seems to me, that directors of social services can not possibly have that feedback. I tried to follow the practice of Harry Mapstone at East Ham: all the child care officers had to do reports, mainly handwritten, and he used to read through a pile of files every day. I did the same for as long as I could. Personal responsibility was written into the 1948 Children Act and I knew I would have to take the can.

The Home Office inspectorate was very helpful. Their periodic visits caused some apprehension but their support when resources were needed from the children's committee could sometimes be a deciding factor. I remember, with gratitude, the opportunity to talk over matters with Percy Tipping who was in charge of the inspectorate at Birmingham. An advantage of having child care under the Home Office was that we did not have to compete at national level with other social services. I remember many Home Secretaries, starting with Chuter Ede, who steered the 1948 Children Act through parliament. Later on, Sir David Maxwell-Fyffe supported the setting-up of family advice centres. At a conference of the Association of Children's Officers, James Callaghan said, "As long as I am Home Secretary, child care will remain with the Home Office." Unfortunately, he did not remain as Home Secretary.

The Association of Children's Officers had some notable presidents, Lucy Faithfull, Barbara Kahan, Joan Cooper, Stanley Allison, Beti Jones, Jane Rowell, Henry Norris, Sylvia Watson, Ian Brown, Harry Mapstone, Kathleen Ruddock with Kenneth Brill as an indefatigable secretary. The association played an influential part concerning legislation. Under the Children and Young Persons Act (1969), children's homes became community homes and approved schools became community schools with education on the premises. Regional planning committees were established in which I was involved. But resources were insufficient to allow ideas to be fully developed.

I did support the Social Services Act (1970) because we all thought it was going to be better for children to be dealt with as part of a family. I now have some regrets about the passing of the Children's Departments. What happened was that most of the new directors came from welfare departments with children's officers as their deputies. But the welfare people did not regard child care as important but as a kind of side show. Child care officers, who became social workers, were sidetracked in that they took on the duties of caring for the elderly and the mentally ill as well. The high standards of child care casework fell.

It is obviously fruitless to think about the possibility of returning to the days of the Children's Departments, if only because of the demands they would make on stretched resources. However, the Curtis Committee's concept of the children's officer, responsible for each child in care or in need of help, was very sound and it worked well. There was the occasional case of a children officer being disciplined perhaps because of a failure by one of his or her subordinates to safeguard the welfare of a particular child. However, over the years I came to know the problems of many children, some of which I dealt with myself. I occasionally made home visits, usually with a member of staff or an NSPCC inspector. On the odd occasion, when alone, aggressive parents had to be handled carefully.

The Children's Departments were important because they emphasized something which has now been lost, the well-being of the individual child. It was this which gave me the greatest pleasure. While I was in Staffordshire, I went to a mayor's reception and a 'beauty queen' said to me, 'I want to thank you for what you did for me." She had been from a homeless family in Dudley and had been a shocker, precocious. But I helped to get them rehoused, she went home and turned out alright. Another time, I was at an adoption conference and I was going down some steps when a man came up to me with a little girl, "We want to thank you for what you did for us. Don't you remember, you dealt with our adoption?" He was so grateful.

Margery Urquhart

Introduction

Margery Urquhart was born in Patagonia, Chile where her father was a sheep worker and her mother a cook. The family returned to Scotland when Margery was eleven and took a small farm near Inverness. Margery obtained a degree in agriculture at Aberdeen University before taking a farm post in Hampshire. In 1936 she enlisted in the Metropolitan Police becoming the first women attached to Special Branch and one of the first women police inspectors in Surrey. After serving as a probation officer in West Ham, she was appointed children's officer of Aberdeen County in 1949. In 1968, she became director of the Social Work Department of Aberdeen and Kincardine and then deputy director of Grampian Region until her retirement in 1977.

Interview

I took over in Aberdeen from Mr Anderson who, before being children's officer, had been in charge of the workhouse. We had in excess of 400 children in care, nearly all in foster homes. I was on my own with no other child care staff. I had to visit all the foster homes and do all the adoption reports. I have just been to the wedding of a girl whose adoption I supervised. I managed because Aberdeen County had ten registrars of births, deaths and marriages and they acted as my assistants. These officers may not have been qualified but they were experienced, caring and constant. I managed to build up contacts with other social service staff. They were few in number so, for instance, if you were in the Peterhead area there was only one probation officer. My police background enabled me to work closely with the police.

The children's committee was good. The chairman was Sir Maitland Mackie who had been at Aberdeen University at the same time as me. But it was a struggle to get more staff. My first request was for a deputy. It was granted and I appointed a woman from the WRNS who stayed a long time. Eventually I obtained a third member of staff, Mary Wilson who was a great, grand-daughter of David Livingstone. She was a qualified child care officer and later became the children's officer for Dumfries. Later still we had area officers, mostly unqualified men, but they did a good job.

Before I arrived, Mr Anderson had been negotiating to start a children's home for twelve children in Aboyne. It opened and subsequently we had more small homes, family group homes in council houses. We also used a voluntary girls hostel in Aberdeen — I am still on its committee. It was unusual in that it catered both for teenage girls and old people: it was amazing how well they got on together. The matron of this hostel went to head up the home in Aboyne. She had direct contact with me and I went out most Sundays. A number of children spent their childhoods in Aboyne. One has served for fourteen years on the staff of one of the royal residences.

We had to work hard. We had to go out to see people rather than them come to us. This might involve walking across several fields to interview people in the fields where they were working. Winter was often difficult, especially in the snow. I recall I remember a snowy walk to the isolated home, in the Peterhead area, of a grandmother who had put money in a jug at the door to ward off evil spirits. She would not allow anyone into the house and her five grandchildren were with her with neither food nor heat. Along with an RSPCC officer, another long walk took us to a farm where one of the boys had gone. On the way, a fall on ice covered by two or three inches of water left me with a very wet, very cold posterior. After work, I had to spend a long time writing up the reports because I felt you had to leave a record of what was happening. So often I did not get home until 10 or 11 o'clock at night. It was the same for the other staff and we had a camaraderie which does not seem to exist today. There was a sense of mission. I could not have left child care and gone to something else. I left the police but I could not leave child care.

One of the first things I did was to start running summer camps for children who were boarded-out. A lot of brothers and sisters were boarded-out separately and in some cases did not know of each others' existence. The long distances meant that often they did not meet. After discussing it with the foster parents, we would bring the children together at the camps and there were some very emotional reunions. Parents could come and visit as well. We ran two camps a year, each taking about fifty children, in country schools. We used voluntary staff; we got some from Voluntary Service Overseas and I recall a very gifted Czech teacher. Some local school teachers also gave their services. We also used some of the older boys and girls as junior staff and that did something for their morale and self-esteem. I slept in the corridor and if they misbehaved they slept beside me. I still meet adults who talk about those camps, it stayed with them. The camps were a short cut to what could take years to reach. There were strong personal links between us and the children. The other day I was talking to a social worker and he said that children and young people do not know where they are today and it can take a year for them to contact all the relevant people to find out. A few months ago a young man knocked on my door. I had placed him in a foster home and now he was trying to trace his mother. He still remembered me and knew where to come.

We had quite a number of children in care because of incest. We stuck to the law and if a child was received because of incest we were likely to prosecute the parents and take the other children into care. These children tended to stay long-term and would only return home if we were satisfied that great changes had occurred in the home. We did not then call it child abuse.

Preventive work was slow to get going in a large country county. But the committee did agree to us paying housekeepers, some of whom were terrific. If a parent had died or was ill, we sometimes put in a housekeeper instead of breaking up the family.

There was a meeting of Scottish children's officers about once every six weeks. I remember Fred Edwards as a very good children's officer although I had to put him in his place once or twice when he shouted at people. Mary Wilson was another. I became chairman and during that period attended the conference of our English counterparts.

When you come to evaluate the contribution of the Children's Departments, you must remember what it was like before 1948. In Aberdeen County, families might well end up in the workhouse. Children's Departments were an improvement on them. The departments provided what a lot of children did not have, a family, safe surroundings, security.

Later, I became director of the Social Work Department for Aberdeen and Kincardine. I thought the new reforms were a good move because it gave access to wider resources and information. In practice, we had difficulty in bringing the services for the mentally ill, handicapped and offenders in with the other services.

Florence Valentine

Introduction

Florence Valentine was born in 1916 in Belfast where her father was a professor at Queens University. The family returned to England when she was three and settled in Birmingham. After leaving school, she undertook the Diploma in Social Science at Birmingham University and then trained as a nursery school teacher. On the outbreak of war in 1939, Miss Valentine was evacuated with the inner city nursery school where she had been teaching. After the school came back to Birmingham, she endured the blitz and then resigned in order to enlist in the ATS and was amongst the first women officers to serve abroad. From 1948-51 she worked for the Kent Children's Department. In 1951 she moved to Cambridgeshire as assistant children's officer taking over as children's officer in 1958. With the abolition of Children's Departments in 1971, she became deputy director of the Social Services Department in Cambridgeshire until her retirement in 1978.

Interview

On returning to Britain, after my war service, I did a year in the personnel section of the Joseph Lucas Company in Birmingham. I could not really stomach it because you had to do what was right for the firm not the person. The Children's Departments were being created so I applied to and got a post as child welfare officer in Kent starting there in July, 1948. The children's officer, Elizabeth Harvie, had been appointed but had not yet started. I was in East Kent, the only officer in that division — there were about ten other child care officers, as we became known, in other parts of Kent. I was given a desk with the education welfare officers and later in the Registry Office. I had not realized how bitterly resented we were by the education people who thought they could have done all the children's work. I was told to find somewhere to live for a giant of a boy, whom nobody could do anything with, who was leaving special school. I did not know where to start but, in the end, a school dinner lady took him in.

The situation was desperate at first and we could only take children into care if we could find somewhere to put them. If it was a small baby I might have to drive to Margate or Birchington where there were children's homes. I averaged about 1,200 miles a month in my old Morris Minor. Many times I had to take a baby home and my mother, who was living with me, would look after it in a drawer until I found somewhere.

I had one girl, aged sixteen, back home after approved school. One day, I was going into our department at the Registry Office when I saw a wedding party entering. This girl was about to get married. I had to go into the registrar and insist it be stopped because the local authority held her parental rights and had not given permission for her to marry. I was not very popular. Miss Harvie, who was a splendid children's officer, came over from Maidstone and saw the girl. She refused to give permission and, after a while, the girl decided she did not want to marry him anyway.

I wanted more responsibility and in 1951 I went to Cambridgeshire Children's Department as assistant children's officer. The staff consisted of the children's officer, Edith Round, myself, one child care officer, a secretary and a part-time typist. The department was in a dental clinic and if you burst into the wrong room somebody was being drilled. Miss Round had an office there while the child care officer and myself were in the old Shire Hall which was not weatherproof and could be bitterly cold. Eventually the Children's Department got its own place in a former residential nursery which had its own garden and space for children to play. But that was turned into an old people's home and we went to a little old fashioned house at 9 Council Hill — it is now an Indian restaurant.

Although I was assistant children's officer, I was a field worker. The other child care officer and I divided Cambridgeshire between us. Being small, it did mean that I could know nearly every child and family. Later more staff came. There was one residential nursery still in the grounds of the old Poor Law infirmary at Linton. It was twelve miles from Cambridge and difficult for parents to visit. There were all these old men around, some of whom were senile. But it had some really good nursery nurses. Later we opened a new residential nursery and were able to close Linton. There was also a children's home taking 15-16 children. Initially it had staffing problems but then we obtained a couple who ran it capably for many years. I remember the wedding of a girl who had been in the home for a number of years she was given away by the housefather. Years later I went to the wedding of her daughter. We often hear about the failures so it was good to meet up with one of the successes.

Miss Round had a breakdown in 1956 and was ill for a couple of years. I carried the responsibility and when she came back I thought, "I'll be able to relax a bit." But she left almost immediately. The children's committee offered me the post. I was unsure as I had applied for a job in Manitoba. The committee persuaded me to take it if only for a few months and I agreed. It was so different when it was my job.

Initially the children's committee had been very old-fashioned and judgemental. They even blamed small children for what happened to them. On the administrative side, you have to learn to deal with the committee. It improved and became very supportive. There was one very difficult case when the child of a Jehovah Witness couple was in hospital and needed its blood changed which the parents refused. We had to go to court to take the child into our care. I spent hours reasoning with the parents and, after the operation, the child went home after six weeks. The committee, and particularly the chairman, backed me to the full through all of this.

I was the only woman chief officer and had thought it would be a great disadvantage, especially as the town clerk, a very powerful figure, was a mason with a "jobs for the boys" reputation. But he was very helpful to me and the other chief officers were very accepting. Later, when my mother was dying, I gave in my notice in order to look after her. The town clerk made me take unpaid leave instead, although he did not know how long I would be away. He was very kind.

We needed a reception centre and the committee agreed to build one. It was at Oakington on the site of an old isolation hospital. It had been ideal for that purpose but not for a reception centre. It was in the middle of fields on a poor bus route which made it difficult to visit. Fortunately, we had a splendid couple in charge, Mr and Mrs Brown. We also built up fostering. Some foster children stayed for long periods but we were also able to develop those ready to do temporary fosterings and to work with the natural parents. These improvements owed much to the increase in staffing I was able to obtain. We had some child care officers who did excellent casework such as Mary Braybrooke and Caroline Dobson. Most were professionally qualified but not all. One was a retired sergeant major: everyone thought he would be awful but he was lovely and afterwards was trained.

In 1965, we were given responsibility for the Isle of Ely. Cambridgeshire had been a small county and putting the two together did make it more viable and powerful and enabled us to provide a fuller range of services. The county was large in a geographical sense and included the isolated fenlands. I did not encounter much child sexual abuse but it did occur in those isolated cottages. I recall one woman saying to me, "It's a fine thing when you can't do what you like in your own home." But it tended to occur in families where there were other problems and we dealt with it as a part of family neglect rather than focussing just on abuse as happens today.

The Children Departments were significant. The Curtis Report made an important statement when it said the children's officer should be 'responsible' for children in care. The legislation made it clear that there was somebody, the children's officer, who carried the responsibility. You were made very aware that you were responsible for every child in care and under supervision. I think that has been lost since the Seebohm Report. I was appalled to see recently that the press named a new, young, hopeful, social worker in court as not having visited a family. I would never let child care officers take the responsibility for what went wrong. This made children's officers so much more careful about everything. With the staff, I would go through every child for whom we had responsibility and see if visits had been missed.

The Children's Departments did produce some great leaders Lucy Faithfull, initially an inspector who inspected me, before she became a children's officer: she was caring about children but not obsessive; always in the battle, good at speaking and prepared to be in public life; she got things moving. Olive Stevenson was not a children's officer but as a trainer she had a great influence and improved the understanding of people who were going into child care. Sylvia Watson was much in the public eye and did a great deal for the cause of child care. Barbara Kahan was always to the fore, very clear with a wonderful mind. Joan Cooper and Denis Allen were others. Today the directors of social services do not stand out. You see one on the box and you ask, "Was that a director?"

Following the Seebohm Report, I did not want to be a director of a Social Services Department. I felt l did not know enough about the elderly and the mentally ill. So I was happy to become deputy to Sylvia Watson until my retirement. I was not enthusiastic about the Seebohm Report, but I don't want to be saying that everything was better in the old days. The new arrangement did give a bigger department. But one loss was that of the Home Office inspectorate. It had more power than when it moved to the DSS. The children's inspectors were accessible and able. You did not feel frightened about being inspected because you knew they were interested and that you would learn about developments in other places. We had excellent help from them.

Sylvia Watson

Introduction
Sylvia Watson was born in 1913 in Newmarket where her parents were regular church goers. She went as a weekly boarder to a school in Cambridge. After Cambridge University and teacher training, she taught in a boarding school and, in the vacations, helped at settlements and on children's camps. With the outbreak of war, Sylvia joined the Ministry of Health as an evacuation officer and then set-up war-time nurseries. After the war she was an assistant education officer. From 1948-1970, she was children's officer for Hertfordshire County Council and then director of the Cambridgeshire Social Services Department 1971-1975. After her retirement she was for many years active with the Save the Children Fund.

Interview
Following the Curtis Report, I became the children's officer of Hertfordshire. The new service brought in untrained people. A number of the children's officers had an education background. I had been an assistant education officer and Joan Cooper had been one in Derbyshire. There were those who had been almoners and a great number who had war experiences, working in Europe with refugees. So, although the Children's Departments did not start with trained people, they did start with a good variety of stimulating people. Joan Cooper was very efficient, quite formidable, she never flipped. Kenneth Brill was an advocate for children. Dorothy Watkins was a personal relationship person. Gwyneth Wansborough-Jones was also formidable but she made a great contribution to child care. Perhaps not being trained had its advantages. They were all pretty well educated with fresh minds but different qualities.

The children's homes were dreadful with, every now and then, a blessedly happy one. I remember two single women who ran quite a small home and who were devastated by the Curtis Report. To them, their children had always been important and they couldn't face going out to the post office as they felt so ashamed that people would think their home was like those in the report. But overall they were awful. We had a ghastly one in Watford, huge, a 100 children in dormitories with not even space for a chair between the beds. Everything done by numbers, quite impersonal — line 'em up, then all to the loo, all to the dining places. They were so grey and so drab, so disciplined. No pictures on the wall except that of the local mayor and council. There was one child who was alleged to have been in the home for a week before anyone discovered him — apparently his mother had just pushed him in.

We were sure we were building the new Jerusalem. We improved material conditions, we cut down the numbers, we treated children as individuals, they got individual clothing instead of going to the local school in a pauper uniform. We eliminated the Masters who kept the cane in the corner, we got more staff and set up new, smaller homes. But at the end of ten years we had not built the new Jerusalem and it was sobering to find that it was something much more subtle. We did make improvements, of that I am sure. But we did not get to the heart of it and haven't now. None the less, they had achieved a personal attitude, a belief in human beings being different and individual.

The children's committee was very helpful. On the whole, what I wanted financially, I got for these were fairly affluent years. At the first committee, I asked for a grant for pictures and then I went out and bought bright, colourful pictures to cheer up the children's homes — and took down those of the mayors and their corporations.

Then we had a great blitz on fostering. For many, fostering was the answer. We learnt something in those first ten years, you may replace a home but you still have this great desire to know where you come from and who you are. For a large number of people, a foster home is only a substitute. Towards the end of that period, a lot of time was spent in tracing who children were, who their parents were. We reunited quite a number. Often that meant just getting them to meet each other. Often it was mothers meeting illegitimate children: they could not keep them but, with a bit of help, they could have them home for a visit. My deputy, John Stroud, was very keen and did much of the tracing. For quite a number, once they met it was enough, particularly those who had been in fairly good foster homes. To know, in many cases, that they really had been loved but it had been impossible for mothers to care was a great comfort to the young people.

Prevention grew very gradually. At first we just were not allowed to spend money on helping parents. I was very much involved in the lobbying for Children and Young Persons Act (1963) which did make it legal.

Every authority had trouble in recruiting good residential staff. We had some good ones. We started with five child care officers and then numbers grew rapidly. They particularly developed fostering. We had some fine officers. I recall Ellen Roberts, she was cosy, just what the children wanted and she loved them. There was Adele Toye. And John Stroud who wrote the novel *The Shorn Lamb*; he was a great character. As the number of staff grew so it grew more orthodox. I suppose training put people more into mould. But it did not grow more impersonal. And it retained a sense of purpose — wanted to wipe out unhappiness, we wanted to cure the terrible evils.

I still hear from some former children. One, in her fifties, writes at Christmas. There was a private foster mother in Bishops Stortford who used to advertise for children, would go up to London to meet mother and child, the child was handed over on condition of no more contact; this woman loved babies and had four to five at a time. As they grew older, she trained them to steal and they were badly treated. We would go to court and the children would be committed to us. One child ran away from this woman in the middle of the night and we got her as in need of care and protection. She is one of these children who still keeps in touch.

In the 1960s, I was one of those who marched up and down the country all in favour of the Seebohm Report. My colleague Miss Valentine was a children's officer who considered it a load of nonsense. She wanted Children's Departments to survive because they were more individual and personal and she certainly did not like the idea of joining the children's service with old people etc. Yes, after the reorganization, a lot was lost. The personal emphasis on children was lost and along with it the training of child care officers. The gain was in being able to look at a whole family, with the granny in the corner. But the Social Services Departments became the dustbin, if there was no answer to a question then chuck in into the social services. The organization has got bigger and more bureaucractic. But it not just Social Services Departments, everything has become more bureaucratic, run by an increasing number of people who take degrees in administration. So the change to Social Services Departments was inevitable, once an idea is born it has to live.

Three

The Achievements of the Children's Departments

The voices of the children's officers leave little doubt that, in little more than two decades, they achieved a great deal. This is not to say that the Children's Departments were without serious defects but their overall impact was such that, a quarter of a century after their demise, their participants are still sufficiently enthused to record what happened. Bringing together their accounts along with other written material, it is possible to identify six main achievements.

The Six Achievements

An Improvement

First, and at the very least, the Children's Departments were a great improvement on the services which preceded them. In 1948, the Children's Departments were created just as the poor law was abolished. For people born subsequently, it is difficult to grasp the loathing with which citizens regarded the mechanisms and the atmosphere of poor law institutions. Nigel Middleton, in his evocative book *When Family Failed*, gives many examples of the sufferings endured by children in these institutions at the hands of uncaring staff and of the institutional effects which occurred even under caring staff. (1971) Children were also cared for by Education Departments, Health Departments and voluntary agencies. Overall, as Eileen Younghusband noted:

> In the pre-1948 services for children it was thought that to provide food, clothing, shelter, education and moral training was sufficient ...
> (children 's homes) were often large, overcrowded, understaffed, barrack-like institutions. (1978, pp. 36-7)

Moreover, the services were often conveyed with the attitude that the children were a burden on the public purse and lucky to get what they did. The Children's Departments were not models of excellence, but their staff did have a greater understanding of the needs of deprived children, which they knew were more likely to be fulfilled in small establishments in which staff communicated to children that they were of as much value as any other children. Barbara Kahan, in her interview, revealed her fierce determination that children in care should no longer have to wear boots that were too big for them. Arthur Leeding told how, in a county which kept a tight rein on expenditure, he did succeed in replacing the semi-circle of institutions, complete with flag pole, by smaller, family group homes. Outside of the residential homes, child care officers were expected to visit foster children regularly, to talk directly with them, to record their visits and to report to committees. The practice of fostering and adoption was raised. Child care did improve.

Personal Care
Second, the Children's Departments carried out a form of care which can only be described as personal. The Curtis Report declared that it placed "great importance to establishing and maintaining a continuing personal relationship between the child deprived of a home and the official of the local authority responsible for ... him." (para. 445) As the Children's Act was going through parliament in 1948, Chuter Ede stated on behalf of the government that the staff of the new departments would ensure that:

> ... in the future much happiness would be created and many promising lives preserved through the skill, affection and attention of those officers. (cited by Packman, 1975, p. 9)

These hopes were taken to heart. The service was to be personal in contrast to the impersonal ones which had existed before. It is noticeable that the children's officers, who were interviewed, often used the word "personal". Children's officers, even those in charge of large departments, often continued to have caseloads. The interviews revealed Joan Beckett insisting on visiting the aggressive, convicted murderer whose child was in care, Joan Cooper and Bill Freeman stepping into the breach in under-staffed children's homes. Members of children's committees visited children's homes and, at committee meetings, took a great interest in individual children. Child care officers regarded the essence of their work not as being in meetings but in spending time with children and their substitute parents. They felt a personal responsibility for the children. I entitled my book about the Manchester Children's Department *The Corporate Parent* because its Children's Committee felt a collective sense of responsibility which made them seek the very best for *their* children. (1996) Yet it was both collective and personal with elected members and staff knowing children by name.

Restoring Natural Parents
Third, the Children's Departments restored natural parents to child care. During the nineteenth century, child care agencies tended to "rescue" children from what were deemed as irresponsible parents. As I have explained elsewhere, practice changed little in the pre-war years of the twentieth century with little effort or belief in either preventing deprived children leaving their parents or rehabilitating them. (1988, chapter 1) Practitioners within the new Children's Departments soon began to challenge these views. Backed by the insights of psychiatrists like John Bowlby in Britain and by research by the likes of Weinstein in the USA (1960), staff increasingly recognized that children's roots were important to them. Sylvia Watson, the Hertfordshire children's officer, wrote that the failing of the Children Act (1948) was that:

> ... it legislated for the individual child in isolation. Children's officers soon found that attempting to wipe the slate clean and rebuild a child's life was rarely satisfactory and that substitute home care, however kindly, was but a pale shadow of the real thing." (Watson, 1973, p. 46)

Strengthened by the Children and Young Persons Act (1963), child care officers put an emphasis both on keeping children with their parents and on reuniting them. As Noel Hustler stated in his interview, "the vast achievement of the departments — in the end, not the beginning — was that families were kept together." Another prominent children's officer, Rosalie Treece, added, "in 1948 children in care were isolated ... we were able to return so many more to their own families."

Even where rehabilitation was not imminent, many child care officers still strove to maintain contacts between parents and children while they were in care. It is true that some houseparents and foster parents found the visits of natural parents upsetting to themselves and the children. Nonetheless, research suggested that regular contact with parents did help children emotionally. In Manchester, the children's officer, Ian Brown — who had himself been brought up apart from his parents — was a strong advocate for maintaining links. In his departments annual report of 1960-61 he wrote of foster parents:

> They appear to be more prepared to accept visits from parents and relatives of children. This not only helps the children to settle happily in their new environments but maintains a continuous contact between parent and child, which is so essential to the process of rehabilitation." (Holman, 1996, p. 87)

The new attitude to parents thus entailed new attitudes from foster parents and there emerged what is sometimes called professional fostering. This term does not mean that long-term fostering went out of fashion nor does it mean that foster parents were motivated by money or desires for status. It was rather that many foster parents began to see themselves as part of the child care team which also included the parents as well as staff of the Children's Departments. Compared with attitudes and practice before 1948, a child care revolution had occurred.

Qualified Child Care Officers
Fourth, the Children's Departments facilitated the growth of trained child care officers. The growth owed much to the backing and money of the Home Office for training courses but this, in turn, depended on the fact that many Children's Departments were eager to recruit trained staff. It must be said that the distribution of qualified officers was uneven with small departments, particularly those in Scotland, losing out to the larger ones. None the less, their numbers grew steadily. Indeed, child care officers became the leading social work occupation. Training for staff in welfare and mental health departments was on a much smaller scale. Psychiatric social workers, often employed in child guidance clinics, were considered a kind of social work elite but their numbers were tiny. Child care was the growth occupation. Debates raged as to whether child care — and social work — was a profession or a semi-profession or neither. What cannot be contested is that child care did constitute an occupation which attracted people committed to the objectives of the 1948 Children Act. Their enthusiastic

commitment continued despite modest salaries, long hours and poor working conditions. As Margery Urquhart observed in her interview, "there was a sense of mission. I could not have left child care and gone to something else."

Child care officers regarded themselves as child care specialists. They attended training courses — and there was in-service training as well as full-time courses — which majored on child care casework and child development. The journals of the time *Case Conference* and *Accord* in particular, were replete with articles about how to select and work with foster parents, how to match children with substitute parents, how to support so called problem families and so on. The deputy children's officer for Hertfordshire, John Stroud, was the editor of *Accord* and also edited a popular text book *An Introduction to the Child Care Service*. Its contents are a good indication of the matters which were regarded as central to child care practice — Reception into Care; Committal to Care; Boarding Out; policy; selection; placement; Supervision; Residential Care; Adoption; Family Casework; The Administrative Setting. (1965) The child care officers thus became a specialist workforce which would have been inconceivable in the 1930s.

The child care officers, as Margery Taylor recorded in her interview, "believed in what we were doing. We wanted to do it not because we set out to become the head of a department but because we believed something needed to be done." This determination was allied with a confidence gained from being specialists. They considered that they had the experience and knowledge to write about and talk about deprived children. Collectively they expressed themselves through the Association of Child Care Officers. ACCO accepted both qualified and unqualified officers into membership but the fact that they contained so many trained members undoubtedly made them a voice to be heard. ACCO played a part in lobbying for prevention to be sanctioned by legislation. As Brian Roycroft explained in his interview, it had the ear of some government ministers. It issued reports and recommendations on fostering and adoption. It had influence on training courses and published its own journals and books. As never before, child care practitioners gained recognition outside of their own ranks.

Jean Packman, herself a child care practitioner before she became an academic, wrote:

The history of the child care service suggests that it is possible to pioneer new methods, even with grossly inadequate resources, if optimism and a crusading zeal prevail. It may be that small and brand new organisations, starting from scratch, can more readily foster such attitudes than a large and complex structure born of a massive merger. (p. 127)

The child care officers had a zeal and skills which enabled them to expand their work beyond children in care and into prevention, family work, offenders. They thus laid the groundwork for ideas about a larger service. Oddly enough, it was this larger service, the Social Services Departments and Social Work Departments which were to undermine the specialism of child care. Oddly enough, as Jean Packman indicates, it was the large and complex structures of the later massive services which were to dampen the pioneering spirit. But more of this later.

Local Authorities and Personal Services

Fifth, and particularly important, the Children's Departments established that local authorities could run an efficient, caring and personal service. During the inter-war years, local authorities greatly expanded their functions. Not only did they become the main providers of education and health services but they also took over utilities, like gas and electricity, which private enterprise was failing to supply properly. However, as the Curtis and Clyde Reports demonstrated, statutory provision for deprived children left much to be desired. The Children's Departments changed all that. Local authorities became the leading child care agencies with a coverage and quality superior to that of voluntary societies and private bodies. Moreover, the incorporation of the personal element, the emphasis on looking after deprived children as individuals, made them different even from the highly regarded Education Departments where the emphasis was on providing services for large numbers. As will be mentioned, the Children's Departments did have limitations. Yet it is worth noting that they had few of the public scandals which became a feature of the succeeding Social Services Departments. The Children's Departments showed that local authorities were capable of running a service which went beyond administrative efficiency and which expressed important human values, in particular the wish to promote the interests of deprived children and their families.

Positive Side Effect

Sixth, the Children's Departments had a positive side effect on voluntary societies. The standards set by the new service pushed the older voluntary agencies into change. In regard to residential care, Children's Departments began to abolish large institutions and to humanize practice. Many voluntary children's homes began to follow suit from a genuine desire to improve their own standards. But it was not just a matter of example. Some Children's Departments insisted on improvements if they were to place their children with the voluntaries. Consequently, the latter also closed their residential villages and began to open family group homes.

Yet change of an even more fundamental nature had to come. As Children's Departments promoted fostering and prevention so the demand for residential care fell. The local authorities then withdrew many of their placements in the voluntary homes. In England and Wales, the number of children cared for by voluntary organizations fell from 25,000 in 1954 to 19,000 in 1960 to 11,500 in 1971. In Scotland, numbers in voluntary homes declined from 5,578 in 1949 to 2,520 in 1969. Apart from residential care, the voluntary societies had also majored in child emigration. In an authoritative article, John Murphy estimates that in the century before 1969, over 150,000 deprived children were sent to the colonies with the national child care societies being the main agents. (1994) Although some emigration continued into the 1960s, it was increasingly criticized on the grounds that children were being needlessly torn from their families and familiar environments.

With residential care in decline and emigration virtually abolished, the voluntary societies lost their two main activities. They responded initially by developing specialized forms of residential care for what were then called physically and mentally handicapped and maladjusted children. Only the largest of Children's Departments had enough children to justify their own specialist establishments and hence the voluntary bodies responded by filling the gap. Similarly, they began to concentrate on showing that handicapped and black children could be placed for adoption. With even more innovation, they turned to prevention. Local authorities gave grants to voluntary bodies like Family Service Units to work closely with families with multiple problems. The national child care voluntary bodies initiated schemes to keep young offenders in their neighbourhoods. They pioneered community projects in deprived areas and so laid the foundations of the path that later led to family centres. The Children's Departments had been created partly because the voluntaries had stagnated. Yet by the late 1960s, the voluntary societies were again pioneering. A positive side effect.

Limitations

There is a danger of exaggerating the merits of the Children's Departments. People like myself can become like old soldiers who, through rose-tinted glasses, magnify the strengths and minimize the weaknesses of the past. It is appropriate, therefore, to identify some of the limitations and failures of the Children's Departments.

The LCC Children's Department was far too large and Denis Allen and Noel Hustler in their interviews, identify many of its disadvantages. But its failings were recognized and the LCC was later broken down into smaller units. Much more common was for Children's Departments to be too small. In Scotland, of fifty-two Children's Departments eight were local authorities with populations of under 30,000. Some boroughs in England and Wales also served tiny populations. Others had larger populations, such as some rural counties in England mentioned by John Murphy, but possessed councillors who were determined to spend as little as possible on services.

The negative outcomes are well illustrated for Scotland in an internal document passed to me by John Murphy in which evaluations are made about departments in 1966. One department was in an authority with thirty children in care and thirty preventative cases; it was staffed just by a children's officer and a clerical assistant; plus residential staff in its one children home; the report commented, "the chairman is interested and helpful but the other members of the children's committee show little interest. The town clerk is helpful and co-operative. The children's officer would benefit from the support and consultation of other professional staff." In another Children's Department in a city, the report revealed that, "the children's officer is having to reside in one of the children's homes because of the shortage of staff and recruitment difficulties." Of another authority, with over a hundred children in care, it was recorded, "the department is numerically well-staffed but is professionally poor and there is a lack of adequate provision for staff in training." Very small and under-resourced Children's Departments had obvious defects as follows:

- The numbers of staff were not sufficient to allow the development of a sense of teamwork. The absence of members through illness or holidays put enormous strain on those still on duty.

- The departments could not maintain a variety of residential provision and hence had to rely on the facilities of other local authorities or voluntary bodies which then led to much time spent in travelling, not to mention having to place children far away from their families.

- They had few qualified staff partly because committees were not ready to release staff for courses and partly because trained child care officers would not join them.

Fortunately, the above type of Children's Departments were the exception not the rule. But nearly all departments had difficulties in maintaining the quality of residential care. Most did reduce the size and number of their children's homes and did try to recruit qualified staff. Some departments did obtain outstanding residential workers. Pamela Mann tells of Meg Plover who ran a family group home with help from her working husband. The Plovers looked after seven siblings through bad and good times and continued to give them affection and guidance when they grew into adulthood. (1984, chapter 2) None the less, there was always a shortage of trained residential staff. Further, rising numbers in care in the 1960s led to some shortage of residential places, especially for children of the Roman Catholic faith. Oddly enough, pressure on residential establishments also stemmed from the increased emphasis on fostering. As Val Scerri explained in his interview, the drive for fostering was pushed so hard that some second-rate foster parents were accepted which led to more breakdowns. He said, "we overlooked the failures, the children who were moved around a lot and suffered as a result." These children, often damaged and demanding, finished up in the children's homes where even capable staff could not cope with them and so they were moved again. It must be said that the Children's Departments did fail these children who were shipped around from one residential fort to another. A graphic illustration of the sufferings of such a victim is found in the published experiences of Graham Gaskin. (1982)

As they grew into adulthood many youngsters stayed with their foster parents until they were ready to set up homes of their own. The position was more difficult for those who were still in residential care when they reached working age. Often their places were required for younger children. Local authorities had permissive powers under the 1948 Children Act to run hostels for working young people but by 1960 there were only sixty throughout England and Wales. Child care officers tried to find them accommodation but their care was never satisfactory. Once they reached eighteen years, the age of discharge from public care, their position could be even more precarious. Looking back on his long experience, Bill Freeman said, "the main limitation was what happened to children after eighteen when they left care. There were very few hostels for them, little back up, we could give them little financial help." Some drifted back to their own families but others had no families to whom to return. Under Section 20 of the 1948 Act, the Children Departments did have powers to provide some after care in the form of limited financial help for maintenance, education and training but later research found that these powers were not widely used. From my own experience, I know that child care officers with a hundred children on their caseloads, opted to give priority to younger children. Visits to working teenagers were squeezed into late evenings while after care was a luxury which time and money reduced to a minimum.

Not least, Children's Departments, like most other welfare agencies of the time, did not tackle ethnic issues. Despite, in the 1960s, an increasing number of black children entering the care of urban authorities, few black staff were appointed as fieldworkers or residential staff. For my book about Manchester Children's Department, I interviewed Tony Hall who, as a young child care officer, had regarded himself as a radical, a fierce opponent of the likes of Enoch Powell. Looking back, he said,

> We all thought we were racially aware — everyone was the same as us. Ha ha. We would uncritically write after interviewing prospective foster parents, "will not take coloured children." We were integrationalists. We thought black people should be like us. (p. 183)

The outcome was that too little provision was made to accommodate the needs of children from different backgrounds and cultures.

Limitations and failures there were. But they are far outweighed by the positive achievements of the Children's Departments. It is not too much to say that child care practice was revolutionized in the period 1948-1971. During the same years, some improvements occurred within welfare and health services. But they experienced nothing like the wholesale changes of the care for deprived children which included the promotion of child care as an occupational specialism, shifts in the methods of looking after children, and the acceptance by local authorities of the noble value that deprived children were of such importance that they deserved the best possible services. There is little doubt that children thrive best if they remain with parents who provide satisfactory care and the Children's Departments, in their latter years, put an emphasis on prevention. But some children do have to live apart from their parents, do have to

112

spend years in public care. Roger Fuller and Olive Stevenson summarize research studies which indicate that children do suffer emotionally by being separated from their parents but that these sufferings can be modified by the quality of their substitute homes. (1983, pp. 67-71) Perhaps the outstanding contribution of the Children's Departments was they improved that substitute care.

An illustration is found in the work of Pamela Mann. A former child care officer, she followed up some of the children for whom she had been responsible in the 1960s and whom she had placed in foster homes, children's homes, with adoptive parents or managed to keep with their own parents. When she visited them in the 1980s, she concluded that there was little doubt that the trauma of their lives had emotionally wounded the children and that the scars were carried into adulthood. None the less, Mann found that most had settled into families and occupations. Nearly all acknowledged the part played by the long-term devotion and skills of their former child care officer. (1984) Write large over the thousands of children who were in care, it can be said with some confidence that the Children's Departments were a power for good.

The Children's Officers

The achievements of the Children's Departments owed much to various sources. They would not have been possible without the campaigners who lobbied for and the parliamentarians who carried through the 1948 Children Act. Following the Act, succeeding Home Secretaries looked with favour upon the new service, although it was small in comparison with others. For some years the Home Office provided substantial financial help for Children's Departments. Within the Home Office, its child care Inspectorate was of particular importance. J. A. G. Griffiths, in his study of the relationship between central government departments and local authorities, contrasts the style of the Home Office Inspectorate with that of the Ministry of Health. The former was seen as regulating through a mixture of firmness and kindness. The latter was 'laissez faire'. The former conveyed the impression that their ministry wanted progress, the latter that it was not too interested (1966). John Moorwood reflected the views of most children's officers when he recorded that the inspectors "were always ready to come and give advice." As a lowly child care officer, I too came across them for, as well as examining policy with the children's officer and children's committee, they examined the case records of individual field workers and accompanied them on visits to foster homes.

Mention must also be made of the children's committees. Initially some were tight-fisted even uninterested. But many became enthusiastic supporters of the Children's Departments. Beti Jones, in her interview, was at pains to pay tribute to her committee and noted that its members took very seriously their duty to act like good parents towards the children in their care. Similarly, Bill Freeman said, "committee members were very important. They lived amongst the people they represented. They visited children's homes, they knew many of the foster children, they knew first hand what was going on. They were a great help."

Within Children's Departments councillors, clerical and administrative staff, residential workers, child care officers and foster parents all played vital parts. Perhaps, though, most praise must be directed at the children's officers. Amongst them there were a number of duds, those who could not cope and were made to resign. None the less, as John Murphy put it:

The role of the children's officers cannot be over-emphasized. They included a large number of able and informed graduate women, and to a lesser extent men, who were committed and crusading activists. (1994, p. 94)

Joan Cooper, one of the best-known children's officers, said, "We had a sense of mission." This mission, which was made up of a commitment towards deprived children, a vision of what could be achieved, and a readiness to work all hours for them, was common to a host of children's officers. They typified child care.

As a student, I worked for several months in the Essex Children's Department where the children's officer was Miss Wansborough-Jones. She was held in awe — her Christian name was never mentioned and never used. When the placement was over, she summoned my fellow student and myself to an interview and quizzed us about our experiences and then she asked us how her department could be improved. I found it remarkable that this formidable woman, with a national reputation, should seek the views of young students and, even more remarkable, that she took them seriously. Subsequently I worked as a child care officer in Hertfordshire. Here the children's officer, Sylvia Watson, was an enthusiastic and inspiring figure. At the monthly meeting for all child care officers, her approach was always pro-active — "how can we improve the lives of our children?" She was also an accomplished administrator and manager at home both with child care policy and practice. I recall her speaking at a national meeting to promote the cause of prevention and then, in the following week, receiving back my records — she read samples of all child care officers' reports — with her comments scrawled across them. Not least, she went to great pains to know her staff and, somehow, always asked after their own children by name. In the course of writing this book, I went to see her after a gap of over 20 years. She looked me up and down and then commented, "Yes, very faded at the edges but it is Bob Holman." She remembered. She was not alone and I hope that the interviews contained in this book do reveal what an outstanding breed of people they were, children's officers who somehow combined idealism with realism.

Four

After the Children's Departments

By the early 1970s, the Children's Departments had disappeared, having been amalgamated in to the much larger Social Services Departments and Social Work Departments. Over a quarter of a century later, the question must be asked, what effects have these changes had upon services for deprived children and vulnerable families?

Significant Changes

The question is difficult to answer because the reorganization of the personal social services has been followed by numerous other changes. The question thus also becomes what is the present state of child care services in the face of the many changes? Amongst the most significant changes in the period up to 1997 have been the following:

Local Government Reorganizations

Since 1970 not a decade has passed without alterations to the boundaries and functions of local authorities. Within a few years of the formation of Social Services Departments in England and Wales, reorganization meant that the 174 departments were reduced to 116, in other words, the size of many departments was increased. Even more radically, in Scotland the fifty-two Social Work Departments were reduced to 12. Most people found themselves living in regions, with Strathclyde Region being the largest local government unit in Western Europe. It is true that Scotland also contained three small island authorities but the trend was clearly towards bigger agencies. The former children's workers thus found themselves transferred not just from specialized to multi-purpose bodies but also from small or moderately-sized ones to very large agencies.

New Duties

New legislation placed yet more duties on the Social Services and Social Work Departments. The Chronically Sick and Disabled Persons Act (1970) and a similar Scottish Act in 1972 placed extra responsibilities upon the local authorities. The 1975 Children Act, amongst other matters, increased local authorities powers to remove parental rights over children in care. The 1989 Children Act and the 1995 Children (Scotland) Act were huge pieces of legislation which included a new duty to provide services for children 'in need'. Terminology was also changed so that in England and Wales children who had been 'in care' were thereafter 'provided with accommodation', while in Scotland 'looked after' referred to children on supervision and/or physically in the care of local authorities while 'accommodated' referred to all children physically in the care of local authorities. Amongst other pieces of legislation, the Carers Recognition and Services Act (1995) gave belated acknowledgement of the needs of carers who looked after relatives at home.

Perhaps the most far reaching Act was the National Health Service and Community

Care Act (1990). It transferred responsibility for the care in the community of elderly, disabled and handicapped people (now more usually called people with special needs) from the health services to Social Services and Social Work Departments. Further, government shaped the nature of provision by favouring a system in which local authorities assessed the needs of applicants and then met them by 'the market'. In practice, many departments split themselves into purchasing and providing sections with the former doing assessments and placing contracts while the latter became the local authority wing which could still offer provision alongside the competition from what was called the independent sector, namely voluntary and private bodies. In 1997, the Conservative government indicated that virtually all provision should be made by the independent sector. In short, the privatization of welfare was underfoot. In addition, some departments began to rely heavily on independent bodies for children's residential provision and even foster care. In urban areas, shortage of social workers and residential workers led to departments using, often on short term contracts, staff from private employment agencies. Later in 1997, a change of government brought the Labour party to power. It is too early to say what changes will occur within the personal social services but the early signs — and the manifesto for the election — do not indicate that great changes will take place.

Social and Political Environment
The changing nature of welfare legislation reflected the changing social and political environment in which child care and other services had to operate. John Murphy puts it well:

... in the 1960s there still existed a firm unchallenged belief in the welfare state, and in the local authority's duties to protect and ameliorate its citizens' lives. By the 1980s government and popular philosophies had veered from these traditional liberal values towards an irresistible tide of hard-nosed individualism and survival on market-place principles in health, education, housing and personal services as well as in industry and commerce. Antagonism to 'professional welfare' implicit in government thinking, was more than matched by open hostility in the media and the market place. (1992, p. 3)

The government insistence that welfare be conducted like business with managers and accountants not professional carers as the key figures, the growing domination of values which emphasized individualism and personal gain, and the vastly increased size of Social Services and Social Work Departments all combined to make welfare agencies more like private companies.

Media Attention
The personal social services became vast agencies and the numbers of social workers multiplied. Accordingly, they increasingly attracted, the attention of the media, particularly in regard to child abuse. Child abuse — physical, emotional and sexual —

by parents, foster parents and houseparents certainly did occur in the days of the Children's Departments. The judgement of most of the children's officers who were interviewed was that it occurred less then than now, although it is impossible to be certain of its extent. However, it is clear that abuse drew less media attention. As I have shown in regard to Manchester Children's Department, it was mostly dealt with by internal action but even official enquiries from outside and even prosecutions drew little comment from the press. Then, hard on the heels of the creation of the new departments, came the horrific death of Maria Colwell in 1973, at the hands of her step-father, after social workers had returned her to her family. There followed some forty public and highly publicised inquiries into the fate of abused children. Frequently social workers were condemned either for returning children to their natural parents or for failing to remove them. A few reports, however, criticized social workers for wrongly removing children on the grounds of alleged sexual abuse. The outcome has been that child care social workers now operate in a climate in which they make judgements not only according to their professional judgements but also with an eye to what the press might say.

Improvements

The references to a political climate hostile to welfare and to the media obsession with child abuse might give the impression that the decades following the reorganization were unhappy ones for child care. But the hostile climate did not come immediately and, particularly in the 1970s, child care improvements were fostered.

Increased Resources and Status

The Seebohm Report had argued that an amalgamation of local authority social services into one super department would enable it to have more political clout and so win more resources. Certainly this prediction was fulfilled in the 1970s. Between 1969-79, expenditure on the personal social services rose from £171 million to £1,641 million on revenue and from £28 million to £68 million on capital. In their first five years, Social Services Departments multiplied their staff by 47 per cent. The drawing of several welfare occupations into one department also led to the birth of the British Association of Social Workers (BASW) which began to forge its media and political contacts. In his interview, Philip Hughes, who was both a children's officer and a director of social services, stated that the amalgamation of services "did lead to a stronger department. Directors are chief officers and I think the Association of Directors of Social Services had more clout than the Association of Children's Officers."

Nowhere were the gains more evident than in Scotland. It had not experienced, to the same extent, the child care crusade of the 1950s. The growth was thus the more marked following the creation of Social Work Departments. Kay Carmichael, who played a part in shaping the Scottish developments, later wrote:

The Social Work (Scotland) Act (1968) was implemented in a wave of enthusiasm a quarter of a century ago. New departments were set up, training programmes offering generic working practices became available all over the country and resources increased by 50 per cent a year. Social Work committees began to achieve political status ... Departments were dealing directly with fuel boards and social work was now at the heart of social strategy policy for a range of disadvantaged groups ... The enthusiasm was palpable. There were striking developments in practice as regions consciously set out to reduce the number of children in children's homes. (1994)

John Murphy, himself a director of one of the new Social Work Departments, agrees and points out that expenditure on social work in Scotland rose from £20 million in 1969-70 to £471 million in 1989-90. Staff numbers escalated and, by 1989, 97 per cent of main grade social workers were professionally qualified. Probably the greatest success, however, was the new system of Children's Hearings which "dealt carefully and sympathetically with a large number of children — some 20,000 annually — with little evidence of serious complaints from parents, public, police or other agencies in a field where, given cause, both press and public are known to be vociferous." (1992, p. 133)

Social Work Developments
The initial availability of resources did facilitate some developments in matters related to child care. Within juvenile justice, the 1970s saw an expansion of intermediate treatment schemes in which social workers used counselling, group work and residential weekends to influence some youngsters away from crime. Other approaches involved close liaison between social workers, police and juvenile courts to slow the rate at which offenders were sent to custodial institutions. Within fostering, foster carers, as they became known, became more accepted as professional colleagues. Isobel Freeman explains how foster carers were used to assess children's needs and as respite carers. (1988)

Within prevention, experiments took place and Richard Fowles depicts how the Strathclyde Social Work Department used sizable sums of money to provide resources for certain families in a successful attempt to keep children with their parents. (1988) A number of Social Services Departments and Social Work Departments also followed the lead of voluntary bodies by setting up family centres which attracted local families. The Barclay Report gave approval to another trend, namely community social work in which teams of statutory social workers were located in areas of high need where they could be close to users and where they could co-operate with residents to set up supportive projects. (1982) Not least, the increasing emphasis on child abuse did lead to social workers becoming more prepared to listen to children's complaints and did promote the setting up of more sophisticated machinery to investigate alleged abuse.

These are just a few examples of the child care gains made within the new departments, especially in their early years. But there were also losses and, during the

1980s and 1990s much concern was expressed about the decline of child care.

The Decline of Child Care

During the 1980 and 1990s, revelations were made about the wide spread physical and sexual abuse of children in residential establishments. It became clear that paedophiles had infiltrated children's homes and, for many years, hoodwinked the authorities. By this time residential care was already in numerical decline and regarded as the last option for deprived children. As mentioned, media focus on the abuse of children within their own homes, often while under the supervision of social workers, escalated from the 1970s onwards. The many enquiries tended to agree that the child care system was failing to protect children.

The Failing System

At the time of writing, the most recent public inquiry has concerned the death of six year old Ricky Neave who, at the time of his death, was on the 'at risk' register of the Cambridgeshire Social Services Department. A report compiled by the Bridge Child Care Development Service, made the following criticisms of the department:

- The low morale of social workers with conflict and poor communication between them and management.

- A high turn-over of staff.

- Inadequate administration shown in files being lost or misplaced.

- Social workers lacking in skills concerning the investigation of the child's situation and in communicating with him (1997).

The report on Ricky Neave reflected criticisms made by several preceding inquiries: faulty communication both within departments and between different social agencies such as the police, schools, health services, and the NSPCC: overworked and dispirited social work staff, a lack of child care expertise amongst social workers: ineffective management systems which meant that some families received insufficient attention while field workers received insufficient professional support. Outside of the reports, child care experts were also worried about the skills of staff dealing with child abuse. Thus Jean Packman concluded, " ... there are many indications that child care practice is failing badly in circumstances where child abuse or child distress is, in fact, preventable." (1975, p. 170) Given that the creation of the super departments was supposed to improve communication and co-operation, to abolish the fragmentation of services, to ensure sufficient numbers of staff and to increase professional competence, these criticisms made sad reading.

The Decline of Prevention

The criticisms concerning child abuse came loudly from outside of social work. Social workers themselves, interested academics and some child care pressure groups were also worried about the decline of prevention — or family support, as it became known. The decline is surprising if it is recalled that the Seebohm Report devoted a whole chapter to prevention; that the Barclay Report identified community social work as a major means of promoting prevention; that the 1989 Children Act and the 1995 Children (Scotland) Act put an emphasis upon it with the later, for instance, instructing to local authorities to:

> safeguard and promote the welfare of children in their area who are in need; and so far as is consistent with that duty, promote the upbringing of such children by their families. (section 22)

Yet decline it has. In 1984, Professor Jane Tunstill stated that Social Services Departments were "paying inadequate attention to the prevention of children being received into care or, once they are in care, being rehabilitated with their own family." (cited by Holman, 1988, p. 57) Throughout the eighties, it became clear that social workers were giving a decreasing amount of their time to prevention. The flowering of community social work enjoyed but a brief summer. Family centres tended to concentrate more on limited numbers of families 'at risk' rather than on being open to whole neighbourhoods. Jane Gibbons, who emerged as one of the leading social work researchers, concluded from a study published in 1990 that social workers "were in retreat from their earlier commitment to prevention." (1990, p. 51) Five years later, in another publication she wrote, "So far at least, the new approach to family support expressed in the Children Act appears not to have had a great deal of influence on the policies and practices of English local authorities." (1995, p. 88)

Criticisms of Child Care Practice

Prevention of family support concerned mainly youngsters who were not in care. Criticisms were also voiced about the standards of practice towards children who did come into public care. Under the new departments, fostering continued as the main means of looking after children. By the 1990s, 65 per cent of children in care were accommodated in foster homes. As mentioned, some fostering initiatives did occur and foster carers were used in more flexible and varied ways. But by the mid 1990s, much concern about fostering was expressed. An authoritative study, sponsored by the Association of Directors of Social Services, the Foster Care Association and British Agencies for Adoption and Fostering, was published in 1996. Having surveyed the work of eighty-four Social Services Departments, it found that 66 per cent had difficulties in recruiting foster carers and that many children were having to be placed outside of their areas so making more difficult any contact with their natural parents. The lack of applications to become foster carers was attributed partly to changes in family structure, with a reduction in the number of two parent households and an increase in the number of working women, partly to the fears of prospective foster carers of the possibility of being accused of child abuse: and partly to the view that fostering had become much harder as children were more demanding. Interviews with 564 foster carers showed that over a half said they were not properly supported by their social workers. In addition, some departments had lost foster carers to private agencies. Shortages then pushed some local authorities into using these agencies, although doubts were expressed about their lack of accountability and their high charges. Simultaneously, a report by the Social Services Inspectorate, based on a study of six departments, revealed that one in eight foster children had been moved three or more times. (1996)

A picture emerged of social workers being unable to give sufficient time to child care practice. The early indications that the Social Services and Social Work Departments would have sufficient resources had disappeared by the 1990s. But it was not just a matter of resources. In a trenchant article, Barbara Kahan drew together current research to criticize the way social workers were carrying out their practice. She established that too often siblings were not being kept together, that placements with relatives — the most durable of placements — were in decline, that significant numbers of children were inadequately prepared for moves, that visits from social workers to foster homes were insufficient and that the foster children were rarely seen alone. (1996)

Adoption practice within the statutory services also came in for some official criticism. A study by the Social Services Inspectorate of sixty-five Social Services Departments stated that a quarter of children for adoption had to wait more than three years for placement. Part of the trouble was that few departments had specialist adoption officers — partly because of a decline in adoption — while few social work managers were familiar with adoption procedures with the result that decisions about adoptions were often made by staff with little training or experience. Although some examples of good practice were noted, the overall conclusion was that adoption had little priority within the service. (1996)

As mentioned, one of the limitations of the Children's Departments was a lack of services for youngsters when they left care. The hope that larger departments with more resources would improve that service has not been fulfilled, even though the 1989 Children Act placed additional duties upon authorities. Research by Bob Broad reveals that the plight of many young people on leaving care is low income, unemployment and inadequate accommodation. Amongst his large sample, over half were out of work. Despite some innovative projects, the overall finding was that Social Services Departments gave little priority and few resources to this vulnerable group of young people. (1997)

Loss of Child Care Skills

Barbara Kahan finished her critique of fostering practice by stating, "we know that since 1975, social workers have often had little specific child care training." She was echoing the views of others about receptions into care, prevention, adoption and child abuse, namely that child care expertise had declined. These fears had been expressed in the early years of the new departments so prompting the National Children's Bureau to set up a working party, with Professor Roy Parker, who had been a member of the Seebohm Committee, in the chair. In its report, it warned of the danger of exaggerating the standards attained by the former Children's Departments. None the less, it stated that "the reorganization of the personal social services ... has led to a loss of the particular experience and skill generated by special and separate local children's departments." (1980, p. 29) It continued:

In our view, the main deficiencies in child care skill and knowledge relate to:

1. insufficient acquaintance with the relevant law and detailed procedures;

2. lack of a close knowledge of children's past and present circumstances;

3. a lack of up-to-date information about the nature and quality of possible resources;

4. an inadequate understanding of the developmental aspects of childhood; and

5. too little first-hand experiences with children and insufficient skill in communicating with them. (p. 30)

In addition, the views of a number of the children's officers who were interviewed — and some went on to become directors of the new departments — was that the personal ethos, the sense of personal responsibility for individual children formerly held by a wide range of officials and councillors, had declined. And with it went much enthusiasm and morale. As one former child care officer and later an area social work manager put it "There was a commitment by the child care officers and other staff; it was a vocation as well as a profession. After the Social Services Departments, it was never the same again." (cited by Holman, 1996, p. 189) Of course, the many Social Services Departments and Social Work Departments varied enormously in their practices and standards. Yet the overall judgement must be that, within the new departments, child care skills did decline as did much of the previously very high commitment towards the cause of deprived children.

Explanations

What explains the loss of child care expertise? As mentioned earlier, the personal social services do not operate in a vacuum and have operated in the midst of significant changes, namely the reorganization of local authority boundaries and functions, the loading of new duties upon the statutory social services, the focusing of media attention upon social workers, and the emergence of a social and political climate which was not favourable to traditional social work. Taking these into account, four factors can be identified as contributing to the decline of child care as follows:

- In regard to social work, the take-over by the generic approach;
- In regard to child care, the domination of child abuse;
- In regard to organizations, the creation of huge bureaucracies;
- In regard to the distribution of welfare resources, the relegation of child care as a priority.

Generic Social Work

The Seebohm Report recommended that, "The present pattern of specialization in employment should be radically altered. As a general rule, and as far as possible, a family or individual in need of social care should be served by a single social worker." (1968, para. 163) The argument was that the Social Services Departments and Social Work Departments would be staffed by social workers who would deal with the needs of deprived children, elderly people and adults with physical and/or mental handicaps — the generic social workers. As John Murphy recorded of the changeover in Scotland:

On the Friday night there were 305 child care officers, 281 probation officers, 276 welfare officers and 97 mental health officers. On the Monday morning there were 959 social workers with shuffled caseloads and naive assumptions that they had been transmuted into generic workers. Those who doubted the transubstantion were not infrequently suspect of heresy, and the workers concerned were often hesitant to pretend other than omnicompetence. (p. 181)

At a gathering to mark the end of the Association of Child Care Officers, Clare Winnicott expressed the hope that child care skills would not be lost within the new social work. But, as her biographer commented, "Certainly, Clare's grief about these organizational changes emerges more clearly than enthusiasm for a unified profession." (Joel Kanter, forthcoming). Her hopes were not fulfilled. Child care expertise depended upon workers having a training which specialized in child care, wide experience with child care cases, and the repetition of basic child care tasks. Generic social workers lacked all three. They received a training which had to reduce the child care content. In practice, they had to give attention to a much wider range of clients.

Significantly, the official investigation into the death of Maria Colwell pointed out that since reorganization, "the average field level social worker, with a wide range of cases has inevitably less experience than her predecessor in the Children's Departments and it may be that less attention is paid in training to this particular aspect of the work than heretofore." (1974, para. 209) Jean Packman added, "Many of Maria Colwell's signals of distress seem to have been overlooked or misinterpreted." (p. 173) They were signals which might well have been picked up by experienced child care specialists.

Over 20 years later, Barbara Kahan saw no improvement in training. She said of social workers, "Their training does not offer the extensive knowledge they need to make wise decisions about complex child care cases ... practitioners have less time devoted to child care in their training courses than they did 30 years ago ... generic training while broadening practitioners' span has inevitably destroyed much specialism and diluted expertise in individual fields of work." (1997)

The Domination of Child Abuse
In time, Social Services Departments and Social Work Departments did return to a kind of child care specialism, although by that time a generation of experienced former child care officers had retired or been promoted to managerial positions where their field work skills were not exercised. However, it was not the specialism of the Children's Departments and was rather one shaped by child abuse.

As mentioned, child abuse was not unknown in the days of the Children's Departments. The difference was that from the 1970s onwards it received massive media coverage and numerous public inquiries both of which tended to heap blame upon social workers. The reaction of central and local government was to make child abuse — or child protection as it became called — the major focus of statutory child care social work. Central government issued frequent guidelines, Social Services Departments and Social Work Departments formed child protection teams, colleges developed child protection training, scores of books and hundreds of articles were published about the topic. The reaction is understandable. The departments had to take child protection seriously, social workers feared the condemnation of the press, and everyone wanted to stop the suffering of children. In fact, abused children made up a small proportion of the deprived and vulnerable children who came under the brief of the departments. Yet it was this small minority which began to shape child care policy and thinking. As David Thorpe concluded from his research, "The new ideology appears to have succeeded in changing the role of child welfare agencies from predominantly one of service provision, to one of policing." He continued, "it's like trying to use an atom bomb to sink a rowing boat." (1994, p. 199) As resources were poured into child protection, so less was available for prevention or family support which had catered for far larger numbers of children. Jane Gibbons noted, "Protection narrowly understood is the dominant concern in work with maltreated children and their families, while assessment of needs and provision of supportive services are relegated to a less important and even marginal role. (1994, p. 199) Family centres, community social work, even counselling for parents with children in need were cut in favour of the intensive concentration on child abuse.

This concentration also facilitated the rise of a different kind of social work which was at once both mechanical and inspectorial — some would say macho. Social workers found themselves having to follow procedures contained in rule books which were almost the size of novels and having to spend hours in meetings with scores of other professionals in order to make assessments about and to review the position of abused or 'at risk' children. Bill Jordan, probably the leading social work academic, regretted that social work has "become more coercive and restrictive with staff checking behaviour, threatening to remove children in order to get compliance like agreeing to attend a centre for training or treatment, and sometimes denying parental access to their children." (1990, p. 3) Adrianne Jones — a former director of social services — and Keith Bilton — vastly experienced in social work, wrote:

> In good child care, social workers and others need to use empathy, intuition, imagination and flair, as well as observation, careful analysis, thought and knowledge. The danger is that the threat of inquiries will pressure them to ensure their own safety by following the rule book ... The dilemma is whether this 'insurance policy' approach, keeping to the letter of ministerial guidance and local policy will produce too much caution and defensiveness. There is a danger that the primary task of social workers may become the completion of standard procedures without incurring criticism, rather than the resolution of childrens' and families' problems. (1994, p. 32)

To sum up. The domination of child abuse has lead to a retreat from prevention and family support which was so central to the former child care. It has also led to a new form of supervisory and inspectorial social work — sometimes called 'soft policing' — which is very different from the former child care casework with its stress on co-operation, positive and friendly relationships with families, support and counselling, in order to enable parents to cope. It is very different from the responsibility given to officers to use their own judgement about families and their own faith in their skills sometimes to take decisions to keep children in their families. This is not to say that the old-style child care has disappeared. It is to say that it is has been overtaken by a different kind of social work.

The Seebohm Factories

With staff in some departments numbered in their thousands, the Social Services Departments were sometimes referred to as Seebohm factories. Like any large organizations, they rapidly developed as bureaucracies with complex administrative systems and layers of management. Bureaucracy is not in itself an evil, it can be a force for efficiency or inefficiency. But the weight of evidence is that within the personal social services it became a source of problems as much as a solution to them. For instance, far from improving communications between different sections, as the Seebohm Report had anticipated, it seemed to make them worse. Jean Packman commented:

> Communications within social services departments must now negotiate a much more complex organisational structure ... Messages pass through more hands and many social service personnel unacquainted with child care matters. The dangers of misdirection, distortion and loss of a sense of urgency become that much greater. (p. 171)

125

It was not just communication between staff on the ground that suffered. Gaps appeared between field staff and managers. Management became an occupation in itself so top managers often had little experience of child care as practitioners. As Barbara Kahan commented, "the management ethos replaced social work traditions and policy makers were separated from front-line workers." (1995) The top managers therefore tended to lack two features which had characterized many children's officers. They did not possess tremendous commitment towards deprived children and they did not — and within huge departments could not — have the personal contacts with children and families. Not surprisingly, the crusading zeal of the former children's officers was not so evident. Staff found themselves no longer in the unity of small teams, cut of from top managers by layers of hierarchies, and missing the inspiring leadership which had come from above. It is not contended that the amalgamation of the Children's Departments into the huge super social services was all loss. But there can be little doubt that their sheer size, diversity and complexity did have some detrimental effect on the standards of and the spirit of child care practice.

No longer a Priority

Following the years of plenty in the 1970s, the personal social services faced something akin to famine in succeeding decades. 1979 witnessed the election of a Conservative government determined both to cut public expenditure and to restrain the scope of local government. Moreover, growing unemployment and poverty, along with an ageing population, placed yet more demands on the social services. Even in Scotland — whose Social Work Departments had prospered for a while — the squeeze on public spending and the worsening economic plight of a substantial number of the population had a detrimental effect. Kay Carmichael commented:

> What we underestimated was the future growth of poverty and the refusal of governments to combat it. Even our unique Section 12, enabling monies to be spent imaginatively for individuals as well as families, was overwhelmed by a sea of financial need.

Departments were less able to cope. John Murphy wrote:

> There certainly were major deficiencies, particularly in urban areas, at times approximating to near breakdown of basic services ... In most (places) there was a heroic struggle by over-burdened and under-supported social workers. (p. 180)

Faced with new tasks, huge demands and a shortage of cash, Social Services and Social Work Departments had to make choices. With government pressure to expand community care, it was child care which lost out. As John Rea Price explained:

> In 1991-92, social services departments in England and Wales spent £589 million more on services for the elderly than on services for children and families. By

1994-95, this had almost doubled to £1,042 million, with the amounts spent on children's services less than two thirds of spending on the elderly. (1997)

Similarly, in her interview Barbara Kahan, who has never lost her close involvement with social work, expressed dismay at the low standards of residential care. She added that local authorities had reduced it not because of any desire to keep children in the community but simply because it was not regarded as a priority and so could be cut. The outcome was to concentrate numbers of very demanding children on the few residential staff who were left. The pressure on child care budgets is also well illustrated around the laudable idea that local authorities should produce Children's Services Plans. In 1995, the government announced it would be mandatory for personal social services, education and health authorities to produce them for 1996. Yet a survey by the Association of Directors of Social Services found that 95 per cent of Social Services Departments had such severe financial problems that they would be spending much needed money on producing plans which they would be unable to implement. Indeed, far from implementing plans, many have had to cut back on child care.

In February, 1997, the convener of the Edinburgh Social Work Department reported that it had 129 children, referred to children panels or in residential care, to whom a social worker could not be allocated. A number of London departments stated that 25 per cent of their child care cases could not be allocated because of a shortage of staff. The outcome was that attention had to be given to urgent crises while withholding resources from the broader band of children 'in need' for whom supportive help could have prevented from escalating into crises. Manchester, typical of many large urban authorities, reported in early 1997 that it was spending nearly £8 million on residential, educational and social care placements for under 300 children and only £4 million on supporting the rest of the city's children in their homes and neighbourhoods. Child care thus lost out in two ways. The overall children's budget received less priority than other user groups. Within child care, resources were concentrated on a small number of highly 'at risk' children while insufficient help was directed at those with fewer immediate difficulties but whose problems could escalate unless preventative action was taken. How different from the days of the Children's Departments when children were the agencies' sole concern. As Joan Cooper put it in her interview "Children's Departments were intimate in a way that Social Services Departments, because of size, can no longer be. Attention was focussed on children and didn't have the rivalry of the elderly, the mentally ill and so on."

The decline in child care can thus be partially explained in terms of the imposition of generic social work, the domination of child abuse, the establishment of huge bureaucracies, and the fact that the personal social services found themselves with too few resources to spread amongst too large a range of different users. If it is added that, in recent years, the growing privatization of welfare services has made many statutory social workers feel devalued and that the major voluntary societies may contract with local authorities to undertake their duties rather than to offer different and pioneering services, then the decline of child care become understandable.

The Survival of Child Care

Child care may have declined but it has not died. There are still social workers who are adept at placing children in substitute homes. Residential care is now receiving more attention. Community social work may be experiencing a mini revival with Peter Durrant and others having formed a Community Social Work Special Interest Group within BASW. The Family Support Network under the leadership of Professors Jane Tunstill and June Thoburn continues to wave a flag for the cause of family support. The deficiencies of generic social work have been conceded with some departments developing new specialisms such as family placement units, youth justice teams and under eights workers. Some training is now available for social workers dealing with children affected by disabilities and those in families affected by HIV. The importance of maintaining links between children in care and their natural parents has been stressed by action research (Masson, 1997). The case for a child care specialism is again being made. In January 1997 *Child Care Forum* hosted a meeting to consider setting up an Institute of Child Care and Social Education. Four months later, CCETSW (the Central Council for Education and Training in Social Work) announced plans for a post-qualifying specialist course in child care. In late 1997, the Utting Report made a strong case for improved standards of local authority foster care, for much closer control of private foster care agencies, and for a revival of residential care with more skilled staff and more precise definition of its functions. (1997)

Policy and Planning

If the above paragraph indicates interest in child care practice, there are also glimmers in regard to child care policy. Consider, Lewisham Social Services Department. In 1985 one its staff members was convicted of sexually abusing a child in a Lewisham children's home. The authority's response was to close its homes and to rely on foster placements and private residential establishments. Recently, Chris Hume, its Director of Social Services has identified the drawbacks of private welfare; placements made via private fostering agencies usually meant that children were transported far away from their own neighbourhoods while they had a high break-down rate; reports on private children's homes indicated "high staff turnover and confused child care practice." Lewisham is thus returning to running its own children's homes with their aims that of rehabilitating children with their parents or enabling them to move on to fostering or independent living. He concluded, "the key point for social services managers is that, provided we have the right procedures and learn the lessons from the various inquiries, it is possible to ensure children are safe in homes run directly by local authorities"(1997). In short, Lewisham is giving more priority to good child care. Likewise, in Manchester, the importance placed on child care is seen in the decision that the children's services strategy group is to be chaired by the leader of the council.

Outside of local authorities, a working group set up by the Gulbenkian Foundation, made a number of recommendations, including one for the appointment of an independent Children's Rights Commissioner (Rosenbaum & Newell, 1991). Another is for a Minister for Children. It may be that, as in the 1940s, plans and proposal for the well-being of vulnerable children are gathering momentum again.

Smaller Departments?

In 1995, Britain under-went yet another upheaval of local authority boundaries and functions. The government introduced 22 new unitary authorities in Wales, 29 in Scotland (plus three Islands authorities) and 14 in England from 1996 followed by another 13 in 1997 and a further 19 in 1998. The overall effect was to bring in more smaller and hence more numerous authorities. In Scotland, for example, 20 of the 29 mainland authorities had populations of over 100,000, eight had between 50,000-100,000, and one was as low as 48,000. In Wales, the populations of the new authorities ranged from 60,000 to 302,000.

The reduction in size of many local authorities, and hence of the size of population served by the personal social services, has its critics. In one of the interviews, Dick Poor made clear his view that very large units, like the previous Scottish regions, could move resources around from rich to poor areas and were also more likely to attract investment from outside. On the other hand, Norman Warner, former director of social services in Kent, points out that many of the well-publicized failures to protect children have occurred in large authorities. In short, the presence of those resources did not lead to their efficient use nor to good communications (1994). Moreover, a report from one of the, new authorities — North East Lincolnshire which was formerly a part of Humberside — declares that the presence of a smaller number of social work managers and field workers has allowed them to draw much closer to users. In York, formerly a part of North Yorkshire, it has been found easier to consult local residents about their needs and views and the department has proceeded with plans to create an adolescent support team and to improve pay and training for foster carers (Cohen, 1996). If smaller departments do make for better child care, then some improvements can be anticipated.

Within the flood of decline, there are indications — in practice, planning and size of units — that the tide may be turning. But it is noticeable that within the new unitary authorities, none has attempted to recreate the Children's Departments. Indeed, specialism is under increased threat. The latest fashion is for corporate strategies and management. If corporate action means officers and members of different departments acting together to plan local authority strategies then no objections can be raised. But it can mean the merging of departments. Already some Social Services Departments have been swallowed by Housing Departments.

Some directors of social services have taken on responsibilities for public health and safety. Not least, Labour's new junior health minister spoke in 1997 of a "reconfiguration" of services and hinted that Social Services Departments could be incorporated into health authorities. The dangers are obvious: social work could come under a chief officer with no expertise in social work; within such departments, social work would be marginalized. Within this trend, there is a possibility that not just child care but social work will be less of a specialism. It is thus timely to record the conclusion of Adrianne Jones and Keith Bilton that

> Problems may arise, however, when there is no powerful child and family-centred framework and ethos holding the sub-specialisms together. Within social services departments, this is evidenced in those authorities where one finds there is no team charged with basic and fundamental support duties under the Children Act, little in the way of neighbourhood or outreach work, and little evidence that the organisation is able to ensure that all its specialist teams maintain a child-centred focus. (p. 38)

Isolated examples of good child care practice, innovative policies produced by a few authorities, and smaller departments are not sufficient to restore child care to its former position. This can only be achieved when, as Jones and Bilton indicate, departments have an ethos of child care, when the cause of deprived children is central to its very being. Proposals to this end will be aired in the final chapter.

Five

A Family Service

In writing this book, I have used interviews with former children's officers to present something of the workings, achievements and limitations of the Children's Departments. In the preceding chapter, I drew upon a number of studies to assess the work of the services which replaced the Children's Departments. Of course, my own beliefs and interpretations will have influenced what I have written and my assessment is that the present Social Services Departments and Social Work Departments have lost something of the child care expertise of the Children Departments. What of the future? How can children 'in need' best be helped? In this chapter I put forward my own proposals and am certainly not writing on behalf of former participants in the Children's Departments — although I know that some are sympathetic with my analysis. My conclusion is that a new social service framework is required which restores some of the strengths of the Children's Departments and which removes some of the limitations of the present personal social services while not overlooking some of their strengths. My major proposal is for the formation of a local authority Family Department which would convey a family service.

Before enlarging on this proposal, I must make clear my belief that both responsibility for, and provision for children and families in need, should rest predominantly with local authorities. As explained, between 1979-97 governments favoured the privatization of welfare services while Social Services Departments and Social Work Departments used a managerial model to split themselves into purchaser and provider sections with one part placing contracts for services and the other half competing with outside bodies to win the contracts. Elsewhere I have detailed my objections to this trend (Holman, 1993). Here it must suffice to draw upon the conclusions of two British experts who have spent time in the USA where the provision of social services is overwhelmingly in the hands of the independent sector. Barbara Hearn examined in detail the purchaser-provider split and discovered that "it had pushed up costs as independent agencies were mainly interested in profit, that users' needs were not met and that the morale of social workers in purchaser sections dropped as they became assessors and arrangers not deliverers of services." (1994)

It must be added that in Britain, as yet, the purchaser/provider system has been mainly applied to community care. None the less, increasing use is being made of private child care services and here it is timely to heed the study by Chris Hanvey which he sums up as follows:

Evidence from the United States indicates that there are at least two major consequences of this mixed economy of care. First, that state services are left with the rump of statutory duties, often provided by staff who are unable to obtain employment elsewhere. This further alienates such agencies from the communities they seek to serve. Second, that it becomes more difficult to adopt a more holistic approach to care. In the case of children's services, for example, a private or even not-for-profit organisation, charged with the task of providing residential care for young people, might discover plenty of "good" reasons why the young person should not be moved on to, say, some kind of family resource. (1997)

The gist of Hearn's and Hanvey's analysis is that a welfare system which is contracted out predominantly to independent bodies is costly and fragmented. Its major emphasis becomes not what is best for the users but what promotes profit or the maintenance and expansion of agencies. Services to prevent children coming into care are neglected because they offer lower incomes than those which place children away from home. In short, the needs of agencies and their owners become more important than those of deprived children and their families.

My starting point is that society as a whole, in the form of public services, should accept responsibility for the care of needy children. These bodies are elected by and so accountable to the public for the performance of their duties in a way which cannot apply to non-elected agencies. They should be the main providers of services because their major concern can be solely for the well-being of vulnerable people and not for the making of profit. Not least, the history of the Children's Departments demonstrates that local authorities can have committees made up of members whose major interest is to promote the cause of their children, can have officers committed to provide quality services for children for whom they have a long-term personal interest. In the same way, local authorities are the best agencies to be responsible for a family service.

The Family Service

The new Family Department or family service would be responsible for the kind of child (and parents) who, in the words of the 1989 Children Act "is unlikely to achieve or maintain or to have the opportunity of achieving or maintaining, a reasonable standard of health or development without the provision for him of services by a local authority." (Section 17) It would concern, to use the words of Adrianne Jones and Keith Bilton, "those children and families who need additional help beyond that which is generally on offer from health and mainstream services" (1994, p. 5). The new department would be responsible for children at risk of physical, emotional and sexual abuse. It would also be involved with those whose quality of life is far below that of the majority of the population, those for whom poverty and social deprivations lead to a lack of social opportunities, those who are excluded from many of the educational, recreational and other social benefits which are enjoyed by the majority of children.

Objectives

Existing legislation already gives local authorities many responsibilities for the children just described. Jones and Bilton draw upon it to list the objectives of services towards the children just described. They are:

- to safeguard and promote the welfare of children in need;
- to promote their upbringing by their families (provided this is consistent with the child's welfare);
- to minimize the handicapping effects of children's disabilities and enable them to lead lives as normal as possible;
- to prevent ill-treatment and neglect of children; and
- to encourage children not to commit offences. (p. 12)

These objectives would continue but, instead of being located within the present, structures which are also responsible for many other user groupings, they would be the sole duties of a smaller service, the new Family Department. In short, the aim of the new service would be to promote the well-being of these children within the context of their families and communities. In other words, the intention would be to make the very best of family life available to as many children as possible.

Structure
The Family Department would take over responsibilities for children while those for elderly people, those adults with special needs, those needing social work help within hospitals and so on would come under a new Adult Social Work Department. Social Services Departments in England and Wales do differ in a number of ways from the Social Work Departments in Scotland, not least in regard to juvenile and adult justice. Having worked both north and south of the border, I favour the Scottish system of Children's Hearings which are serviced by local authority social workers and of social work supervision of adult offenders. Space forbids deeper discussion here but I would advocate the replacement of youth courts in England and Wales by a hearings system whose decisions would be carried out by the officers of the Family Departments. Lastly, I would put an additional responsibility on to the new service, making it take over the running of youth services (often called youth and community work services in Scotland) from existing departments, usually Education Departments. My reasoning is that youth services, sadly neglected in many local authorities, can play an important part generally in improving the quality of life for young people and, more specifically in reducing delinquency and preventing family break-ups. (See, Holman, 1995)

Which government ministry should oversee the new Family Department? The obvious choice would seem to be within those ministries responsible for health, social security, education or adult social work services. My fear is that children's services would be sidelined within ministries with other major duties. My choice would be to place it within the Department of the Environment (and the corresponding minister in the Scottish Office) for two reasons.

First, because within a comparatively small department the needs of families would receive priority. Second, because it lends itself to a philosophy of care which is that the new service should create a social environment which allows parents to cope and children to prosper.

Interestingly, the concept of a family service is not completely new. Indeed, the Seebohm Committee was supposed to make proposals for "an effective family service". In their submissions to that committee both the Association of Children's Officers and the Association of Child Care Officers wanted a family service to which adult services would be added at a later stage. Their fear was that wholesale amalgamation of the personal social services would lead to the decline of specialist services for children. Their fears were fulfilled and, over a quarter of a century later, it is timely not to go back to Children's Departments but to create Family Departments to stand in their own right quite separate from other services.

Approaches

Structures are necessary but not sufficient. I am a football freak and I know that the sport could not function without the ordinances which determine the number of players in the teams, the size of pitches and the rules of the game. But, in addition, successful teams have to apply tactics, methods, ploys, which can collectively be called "approaches to the game". In like manner, Family Departments must have structures and duties prescribed by legislation. But success will also depend on the methods or approaches they adopt in order to achieve their objectives. The following would be crucial.

A Family-Centred Approach

The Children's Departments started with a child-centred approach in which committees and staff were inspired by the belief that deprived children deserved the best service possible. This vision was not lost but by the 1960s it was merged into a family-centred approach in that children's interests were regarded usually as best served if they were enabled to stay with their own families. To this end, child care officers attempted to strengthen families by providing emotional and material support. Of course, child care officers sometimes did have to remove children from unsatisfactory homes but generally — as Pamela Mann shows in her account of her child care practice — they were not seen primarily as a threat but often as a friend to the family (1984).

The same approach should prevail in Family Departments. The social work staff, they can be called family workers, would regard their primary aim as not to remove children to a different environment but rather as enabling children to stay with their own parent or parents. To this end, the departments would be able to offer home helps, family aids, day care and other supporting services. These would be co-ordinated by the family workers who would also be equipped with what Clare Winnicott called the skills of child care casework, the ability to help parents understand their problems along with the warm support that sometimes encouraged them to persist as parents. And, when children do have to leave home, these skills can be employed to communicate sensitively with them in order to explain, if possible, the reasons for what is happening, to prepare them for the next steps, and to maintain positive links with home.

This is not to undermine the skills developed by child protection staff nor to deny that children must be protected from abuse. It is rather to state a shift of emphasis, to make the maintenance of satisfactory family life the priority.

A Community Approach
The kind of intensive support and involvement, as described above, would apply to families whose difficulties have reached the point where regular involvement with a family worker is necessary. But it is also envisaged that family workers and other staff would have dealings with a much broader band of the community for their departments would adopt a community approach. Family workers and other staff would be based in neighbourhood teams, particularly in socially deprived areas. Their location would make them known to and available to local families, enable them to be familiar with local teachers, medical personnel, policepersons and other resourceful figures. These contacts would give the family workers insights into the ways in which families' behaviour and needs are shaped by the conditions and dynamics of the area and also equip them with knowledge of what local resources are on hand.

As mentioned in chapter four, this approach has been called community social work. Perhaps it can be retitled neighbourhood family work. But it should not limit staff to working just with individual families. In recent years, residents of deprived areas have often formed neighbourhood groups which provide credit unions, food co-operatives, play schemes, community transport, welfare rights advice, youth clubs, holidays and so on. Elsewhere, I have explained that over two million people participate in these locally controlled activities (Holman, *FARE Dealing: Neighbourhood Involvement in a Housing Scheme,* 1997a). These groups tend to be supportive of those with low incomes for by providing cheap food, low credit, holidays, youth clubs, they often relieve stress on hard-pressed families. Moreover, by providing opportunities for unemployed persons, single parents, those who feel socially excluded, to take on leadership roles they often boost their self-confidence. I recall a single mother whose child was in care who joined and then became the chair of a food co-operative in Easterhouse, Glasgow. The new status, the discovery that she had more talents than she realized, the improved self-image, not only made her a valuable volunteer, it also appeared to improve her capacities as a parent. In short, neighbourhood groups have something in common with the proposed Family Departments. It follows that an important role of family workers would be to back neighbourhood groups.

A Facility Approach
The Seebohm Report recommended that Social Services Departments should serve the

population at large and would be an open door to acceptable services. The recommendation was ignored by the government and so did not feature in legislation while, in practice, the eventual shortage of resources and the concentration on child abuse meant that the public often perceived child care services as being for inadequate or even dangerous families. I recall a needy lone mother in Easterhouse refusing point blank to approach social workers for help for fear that her children would be removed. I do not think her fears were entirely justified but her perception reflected that of others who mistakenly called social workers 'child snatchers'.

Family Departments would be different. They would offer some services — such as youth clubs, day care for prefives and family centres — to whole neighbourhoods. These are services which are not only supportive of families but which are acceptable to them. In my study *Children and Crime*, I point out that well-run youth clubs can provide constructive leisure for a whole range of youngsters while at the same time can steer a minority, who are at risk of offending, away from delinquency (1995, part two). Reviewing the research about services for young children, Crescy Cannan concludes that high quality statutory day care centres and nurseries are of benefit to both the children and their parents. However, many local authorities have restricted their use to families where abuse has or is likely to occur (1992, pp. 144-49). The new family service would offer youth clubs, play schemes, holidays and day care to all residents. Users would include families with severe problems but would not be restricted to them. Consequently attendance would cast no stigma on users.

Similarly with family centres. The 1989 Children Act described family centres as places where family members may attend for occupational, social, cultural or recreational facilities and for advice, guidance or counselling. Two main kinds of family centres have developed. The client-focussed type has concentrated on treating small numbers of abused (or 'at risk') children and their parents. The neighbourhood type has been open to whole communities offering facilities such as preschool play groups, after-school clubs, women's groups and educational classes. A study by Gibbons and her colleagues suggest that neighbourhood centres attract local involvement including families in need (1990). It is this kind of centre which Family Departments would promote.

One of the interesting findings about neighbourhood family centres run by voluntary agencies is that residents who initially approached for help with their difficulties may ultimately become helpers themselves (Holman, 1988, p. 179). This outcome has been confirmed in a detailed study by Karen Thomson in Australia. Her doctoral thesis examined the interaction between the unqualified staff at a voluntary centre and users. The former had often been users themselves, had experienced social deprivations and family difficulties, but had endured to become full-time staff members. Their backgrounds and experiences eased their communication with present users and enabled them to convey positive messages of encouragement which improved the latter's functioning (1997). The new Family Departments should finance voluntary facilities of this kind.

Family Departments would serve a broad range of families, particularly in areas of social deprivation where they would make available the amenities that enable more families to cope on their own. None the less, there would still be some families who for various reasons — perhaps because of exposure to long-term stress and poverty, perhaps because of inbuilt emotional difficulties in making relationships — reach the point when family life is at risk of disintegration. In response, Family Departments should mount a three-fold approach as shown in the following diagram:

Neighbourhood facilities

Community involvement

Family-centred

Figure 1: A three-fold approach

Neighbourhood facilities would ensure that broadly-based services like youth clubs, day care, family centres, would be available to all residents who chose to go to them. These facilities would be both provided directly by the local authority and by voluntary agencies. Next, the community approach would contain a double-fold form of involvement; the family workers and other staff would participate in local activities so as to be recognized as positive and helping figures; local neighbourhood groups would be grant-aided to encourage residents to be involved in self-help groups to strengthen the quality of people's lives. Not least, family workers and other welfare staff would be on the spot for families requiring more individual support, counselling or intervention. The users would understand that the main aim of the family workers, whom they would probably already know, would be to maintain family life. But if it did become necessary to place children in foster, children's or adoptive homes, they would be assured that action was being taken by family workers who understood them, their children and their social conditions and who also were expert, by virtue of training and experience, in child care.

Objections

The proposal for a family service makes a radical turn in the trend of welfare developments over the last three decades. It calls for smaller agencies not larger empires, it wants more specialism and less generalism. It is sure to provoke criticisms from vested interests, particularly from those whose personal status, sense of power and large salaries depend upon having huge departments. In addition, more serious and more honourable objections will be raised. Three are as follows:

Too Small to be Effective

The new Family Departments would probably be half the size of the present Social Services Departments and Social Work Departments. Moreover, recent reforms of local authority boundaries mean that many would be serving populations of 50,000-150,000. The objection will be that such scaled down departments will lack the resources to run a comprehensive variety of child care services while they will lack the political clout and influence of the present super departments.

It must be acknowledged that the very large Social Services Departments and Social Work Departments did have the advantages of being able to move resources around. In Scotland, in the enormous Strathclyde Region, the Social Work Department did give priority to deprived parts as against the more affluent suburbs. However, the disadvantages of huge bureaucracies have already been discussed as has the point that, for all their political clout, these departments have not won sufficient resources. The history of the Children's Departments shows that some small departments did have considerable political influence and did succeed in constantly increasing their budgets. In other words, their influence depended not so much on their size as on the public standing of chief officers and committee members who were wholly committed to the cause of deprived children.

The Family Departments would be smaller but not small. If their staff are half the number of present Social Services Departments and Social Work Departments then most would have at least a hundred social work staff plus those staff who formerly were in the youth service. Annual budgets, at today's prices, even in a small unitary authority such as Bournemouth would be about £14 million with others far in excess of that. Could they provide a variety of child care services? Barbara Kahan points out that, by the end of the 1960s, many Children's Departments, far smaller than the proposed Family Departments, had achieved a balance between foster care and residential care and that within the latter a number had a mix of medium-sized homes and family group homes (1995). It may be that departments in the very smallest authorities, such as Rutland, would have to make joint user arrangements for some specialized residential services. Even so, similar joint arrangements frequently worked well in the days of Children's Departments. Interestingly, Cohen and Rea Price point out that the Nordic countries provide local authority children's services within units far smaller than in the UK. The services are of a high standard, give priority to families and their children, and are well regarded locally (1996). Lastly, it may be that the new service with its emphasis on the value-laden word 'family' may prove attractive to politicians so as to ensure that the new family committees have their share of able members.

Difficulties in Communication

Another objection will be that the creation of an extra local authority service will make for difficulties in communication with other departments and agencies. It will be argued that the splitting up of the super departments will nullify the intent of the

Seebohm Report, which declared that the amalgamation of services would ease communication. Yet, as numerous official inquiries into child abuse cases have shown, the amalgamated departments often failed to liaise effectively not only with outside agencies but within themselves. Size became a barrier. In his study, David Cooper asserts that, at local levels, officials from smaller agencies liaise better than numerous officials from the same department (1993, pp. 106-7). The fact that their agencies have less comprehensive but more clearly defined objectives appeared to give them a confidence in what they were doing and what to communicate. This certainly accords with my own experience in recent years in a small neighbourhood project. Our staff communicate freely with teachers, health visitors and housing officers because their paths frequently cross in the same area and face-to-face contact is maintained with persons whose names are known.

Loss of Mental Health Expertise
A third objection will focus on mental health. Mental health professionals, it will be argued, are likely to stay within the adult services with the result that their experience and expertise will be lost to children and families. Yet there is no reason why Family Departments should not employ psychiatrists who specialize in work with children. Further, it must be recalled that training courses for child care officers usually had a strong input from psychiatrists, psychologists and psychiatric social workers who taught what was called 'child development'. The course I attended at the LSE had teaching from Donald Winnicott and Stewart Prince, both eminent psychiatrists. Far from diluting knowledge of mental health, a return to more specialist child care training should strengthen it.

For a Family Department
Without denying that a family service would have some limitations these would be out-weighed by the following advantages.

A Clear Focus
The account of the Children's Departments showed that one of its main strengths was its clear aim of improving the lot of deprived children. It was an aim with which staff and councillors could easily identify and one which could be understood by outsiders. By contrast, the Social Services Departments and Social Work Departments cover so many client groupings and so many needs that both staff and public are unsure about its focus with the result that both its aims and methods seem nebulous. The new Family Departments would have the clear aim of ensuring that the benefits of family life are available to as many children as possible. Elected members and staff would be drawn together by this straightforward aim which would be regarded positively by society at large.

Benefits of Moderate Size
Second, some benefits would stem from the moderate size of the new departments. As

mentioned, a number of Children's Departments were too tiny to be effective. Yet, within those of modest size, there can be little doubt that the high morale of children's officers and child care officers sprang from the unity of small teams committed to a common purpose conveyed through personal relationships. These virtues were often lost in the huge bureaucracies that swallowed them up.

In terms of size, of staff numbers and budgets, the local authority Family Departments would be somewhere between the Children's Departments and the Social Services and Social Work Departments. Hierarchies would be less in evidence, the family services director would be known to and more accessible to staff, paper work would be reduced. Committee members would again know about some users as individuals. Given that much of the work would be based on neighbourhoods, it can be anticipated that managers would have closer links with users and that teams would be small enough for members to relate closely with each other. Something of the personal element could be restored.

Family Support
Third, the new service would be strong on family support. It was shown that family support or prevention is not a priority within many Social Services Departments and Social Work Departments. But in Family Departments, where children's services would not be competing with those for adult community care, they would receive priority. Moreover, with the major aim being to uphold healthy family life, the promotion of positive parenting and the prevention of children having to enter care would be in the forefront of policy and practice.

Family support would be strengthened by the approaches of neighbourhood facilities and community involvement. Open facilities like day care and youth amenities would provide more parents and children with the resources to cope. Community social work — or neighbourhood family work as I prefer to call it — would enable staff to help some families early before difficulties grew into crises. In Oldham, Steve Rogowski led a team of community social workers and found that eventually official referrals dropped by 85 per cent while informal callers rose markedly. Significantly, reports show that such work is not at the cost of neglecting child abuse cases. In Rotherham, the Social Services Department experimented by placing a small team of social workers in a disused community centre on a neglected council estate; the team, led by Derek Eastham, supported residents in running youth clubs and educational classes and became trusted figures to whom individuals could turn; the numbers of children in care dropped while those on the 'at risk' register declined to almost zero (Holman, 1993, p. 75). Similarly, Norma Baldwin and Nick Spencer concluded from their review of the literature:

> community wide strategies aimed at supporting all child carers are more likely to succeed in preventing child abuse than those based on identification of 'high risk' groups. (1993)

The part of locally run neighbourhood provision is also clear. As Jane Gibbons and her colleagues concluded from their study of prevention, "parents under stress more easily overcome family problems ... when there are many sources of family support available in local communities"(1990, p. 162).

The strategy of offering facilities, working within neighbourhoods and promoting community involvement will support families for three main reasons. First, it will attempt to do something about the social deprivations which damage the lives of poor people; family workers using their welfare rights knowledge to ensure that families receive their full entitlements; managers directing grants to families and groups; the staff of family centres boosting the confidence of parents under pressure; neighbourhood groups providing practical services. Second, it will convey to residents that their hope is to keep families together not to disrupt them. Third, it will mean that family workers are on the spot, are known to and trusted by parents and youngsters who are facing severe personal difficulties.

Acceptable to the Public

Fourth, the new service should be acceptable to the public at large. John Rea Price points out that the Seebohm vision was for "a comprehensive family service ... Its universal nature would preempt the stigmatization, now so familiar, of those who called upon or required its support." (1997) As Rea Price indicates, the vision was never fulfilled. The domination of child protection resulted in some parents being afraid to approach social workers for help for fear that their children would be removed. The Family Departments would be different. Their clear mission would be to preserve families. Priority would go to family support. Many of the facilities would be ordinary in the sense that they would be open to any families not those marked out as 'inadequate', 'dangerous' or 'delinquent'. This is not to say that family workers would never be criticized for failing to remove children or for removing them unnecessarily. It is to say that this would occur in a context in which services are regarded much more positively than at present.

Child Care Specialism

Fifth, the benefits of child care specialism would be restored. Family workers would not be generic social workers: they would not spend much of their working lives sitting at desks, ticking little boxes, making assessments and acting as mini accountants. A large amount of their time would be spent with families in varying degrees of need, ranging from those who require linking up with local networks, to those who need frequent support and encouragement, to those who need regular counselling about their personal problems, to those whose children — for their own safety or development — may require placements in residential care or with substitute families. Their continued contact with families, their repetition of similar child care tasks, their growing experience of communicating with children, will make them child care specialists within the context of families. They would display many of the skills of the former child care officers yet it would not be a return to Children's Departments for the family service, to a far greater extent, would be located in and would offer facilities to neighbourhoods. Family workers would be specialists in making relationships but they would be relationships with communities and with neighbourhood groups as well as with parents, young people and children.

Idealism and Realism

I am putting forward a kind of vision, a desire to promote the best possible lives for families, especially for those children and parents who are numbered in what Will Hutton calls the excluded 30 per cent of our society, those who tend to survive on low wages or state benefits, those who dwell in the inner cities and neglected council estates (1995, chapter 8). My hopes may well be dismissed as too idealistic both on the grounds that radical change can not be expected in contemporary Britain and also because so many parents do not care about their children. My answers must spring from experience. When I was born, Britain had no statutory children's service, no specialist child care officers, little public discussion of the needs of deprived children. By the time I was twelve, a new, humane and great public service, the Children's Departments had come into being. Change is possible. Then, for the last twenty-one years I have lived and worked in deprived areas so I know what life is like at the hard end. I am a realist. I am convinced that nearly all parents want the best for their children and want to look after them properly; I am sure that nearly all children want to stay with their own parents and enjoy safe and secure upbringings in their own communities. I am proposing the creation of local authority Family Departments because they could promote these ends. Of course, Family Departments are not sufficient. As I have argued elsewhere, the foundations of a better and more just society must depend upon structural reforms which distribute income, wealth and power more equitably. (1997b) Yet these changes are not completely separate. Both depend upon the spread of different values and, in particular, a belief that all citizens should have fair access to the country's resources and opportunities.

Objections would also be raised on the grounds of costs. It will be argued that the proposed family service will cost far more than what present day services are spending on children and that the current political climate is for a reduction not an expansion of state expenditure. The claim is probably true for the Family Departments will be offering facilities to whole communities. Yet Britain is an affluent society. To draw upon Will Hutton again, his book *The State We're In* demonstrates that the incomes and wealth of 40 per cent of the population have increased dramatically in recent decades in years in which they have paid proportionately less tax. The number of millionaires in Britain has risen steadily. At Christmas 1997 it was estimated that dealers in the city of London received bonuses totalling one million pounds. The money is there, the political will to tax and distribute it is not. The 1948 Children Act replaced the Poor Law philosophy that deprived children should be treated meanly, with the belief that they should have the same opportunities as other children. This belief was widely accepted and public money from local and central government was forthcoming to implement it. Today we urgently require the proclamation of the value that all citizens are of equal value and that society's resources should be pooled in order to improve the quality of family life of those who are made to lag behind. Our politicians constantly say that good family life is the backbone of the nation. In that case, they should be willing to spend resources to ensure that far more children can stay with their families. And society as a whole should be ready to distribute its material, social and emotional benefits amongst all children, amongst all families.

Bibliography

T. Ainsworth, *Sydney Black*, (Book and Tract Depot, 1911)

M. Allen, *Memoirs of An Uneducated Lady*, (Thames and Hudson, 1975)

N. Baldwin and N. Spencer, "Deprivation and child abuse: implications for strategic planning in children's services", *Children and Society*, 7, 4, 1993

M. Barnes, *Curtis to Seebohm*, (private publication, 1980)

J. Bowlby, *Maternal Care and Mental Health*, (World Health Organisation, 1951)

J. Bowlby, *Child Care and the Growth of Love*, (Pelican, 1953)

Bridge Report, *Report of the Bridge Child Care Development Service on Ricky Neave*, (Cambridgeshire SSD, 1997)

K. Brill, *The Curtis Experiment*, Ph.d thesis, (University of Birmingham, 1991)

B. Broad, *Young People Leaving Public Care*, (Jessica Kingsley, 1997)

B. Bulpin, *The Foster Carer Market: A National Perspective*, (Association of Directors of Social Service, 1997)

C. Burt, *The Young Delinquent*, (University of London Press, 1925)

A. Calman, *Life and Labours of John Ashworth*, (Tubbs and Brook, 1875)

C. Cannan, *Changing Families: Changing Welfare*, (Harvester Wheatsheaf, 1992)

K. Carmichael, "Great Scots", *Community Care*, (17-23 November, 1994)

M. Carson, "Glasgow's pride and problem", *Glasgow Herald*, (21 July, 1950)

Clyde Report, *Report of the Committee on Homeless Children*, Cmd. 6911 (HMSO, 1946)

B. Cohen and J. Rea Price, in K. Tidsall (ed.), *Child Welfare*, (HMSO, 1996)

P. Cohen, "Not all child's play", *Community Care*, (21-27 November, 1996)

D. Cooper, *Child Abuse Revisited*, (Open University Press, 1993)

Curtis Report, *Report of the Care of Children Committee*, Cmd. 6922 (HMSO, 1946)

D. Donnison, *The Neglected Child and the Social Services*, (Manchester University Press, 1955)

R. Fowles, "Preventing reception into care", in I. Freeman and S. Montgomery (eds.), *Child Care: Monitoring Practice*, (Jessica Kingsley Publications, 1988)

D. Fraser, *The Evolution of the British Welfare State*, (Macmillan, 1973)

I. Freeman, "The changing role of foster parents in temporary placements", in

I. Freeman and S. Montgomery (eds.) *op. cit.*

R. Fuller and O. Stevenson, *Policies, Programmes and Disadvantage*, (Heinemann, 1983)

G. Gaskin, *Gaskin*, (Jonathan Cape, 1982)

J. Gibbons *et al.*, *Family Support and Prevention*, (HMSO, 1990)

J. Gibbons, "Family support in child prevention", in M. Hill, R. Hawthorne Kirk and D. Part, *Supporting Families*, (HMSO, 1995)

J. A. G. Griffiths, *Central Departments and Local Authorities*, (Allen and Unwin, 1966)

C. Hanvey, "US exemplifies consequences of the mixed economy of care", letter to *Community Care*, (27 March-2 April, 1997)

D. Haynes, *Haste Ye Back*, (Jarrolds, 1973)

B. Hearn, "The purchaser/provider split, 15 years on", *Concern*, (no. 88, 1994)

J. Heywood, *Children in Care*, (Routledge and Kegan Paul, 1959)

J. Heywood and M. Allen, *Financial Assistance in Social Work*, (Manchester University Press, 1971)

B. Holman, *Trading in Children. A Study of Private Fostering*, (Routledge and Kegan Paul, 1973)

B. Holman, *Putting Families First*, (Macmillan Education, 1988)

B. Holman, *Good Old George: The Life of George Lansbury*, (Lion Publishing, 1990)

B. Holman, *A New Deal for Social Welfare*, (Lion Publishing, 1993)

B. Holman, *The Evacuation: A Very British Revolution*, (Lion Publishing, 1995)

B. Holman, *The Corporate Parent; Manchester Children's Department 1948-1971*, (National Institute for Social Work, 1996)

B. Holman, *FARE Dealing: Neighbourhood Involvement in a Housing Scheme*, (Community Development Foundation, 1997a)

B. Holman, *Towards Equality: A Christian Manifesto*, (SPCK, 1997b)

Home Office, Circular 258/52, (November, 1952)

C. Hume, "Good homes of our own", *The Guardian*, (8 January, 1997)

W. Hutton, *The State We're In*, (Jonathan Cape, 1995)

Ingelby Report, *The Report of the Committee on Children and Young Persons*, Cmd. 1191, (HMSO, 1960)

S. Issacs (ed.), *The Cambridge Evacuation Survey*, (Methuen, 1941)

A. Jones and K. Bilton, *The Shape of Children's Services*, (National Children's Bureau, 1994)

B. Jordan, *Social Work in an Unjust Society*, (Harvester Wheatsheaf, 1990)

B. Kahan, "The child care service", in P. Townsend and others, *The Fifth Social Service*, Fabian Society, 1970

B. Kahan, "Simply the best", *Community Care*, (30 March-5 April, 1995)

B. Kahan, "Public parenting", *Child Care Forum*, (May, 1996)

B. Kahan, "None so deaf...", *Child Care Forum*, (July, 1997)

J. Kanter, *Clare Winnicott: her life and legacy*, (forthcoming)

Kilbrandon Report, *The Report on Children and Young Persons (Scotland)*, Cmd. 2306, (HMSO, 1964)

M. Knapp and E. Robertson, "The cost of services", in B. Kahan (ed.), *Child Care Research, Policy and Practice*, (Hodder and Stoughton, 1989)

McBoyle Report, *Report of the Committee on the Prevention of the Neglect of Children*, (HMS0, 1963)

P. Mann, *Children in Care Revisited*, (Batsford, 1984)

Maria Colwell Report, *Report of the Committee of Inquiry into the Care and Supervision Provided in Relation to Maria Colwell*, Department of Health and Social Security, (HMSO, 1974)

J. Masson, C. Harrison and A. Pavlotic, *Working With Children and Lost Parents*, York Publishing Services, 1997)

N. Middleton, *When Family Failed*, (Gollancz, 1971)

Monckton Report, *Report on the Circumstances which led to the boarding out of Dennis and Terence O'Neill at Bank Farm, Minsterely and the steps taken to supervise their welfare*, Cmd. 636, (HMSO, 1945)

J. Murphy, assisted by G. McMillan, *British Social Services: The Scottish Dimension*, (Scottish Academic Press, 1992)

J. Murphy, "One hundred years of child care by emigration 1869-1969", (*SCOLAG*, 28 February, 1994)

J. Packman, *The Child's Generation*, (Blackwell and Robertson, 1975)

R. Parker (ed.), *Caring for Separated Children*, (Macmillan, 1980)

R. Parker, "The gestation of reform: the Children Act 1948" in P. Bean and S. MacPherson (eds.), *Approaches to Welfare*, (Routledge and Kegan Paul, 1983)

J. Rea Price, "Losing hands down", *The Guardian*, (12 February, 1997)

M. Rosenbaum and P. Newell, *Taking Children Seriously*, (Gulbenkian Foundation, 1991)

Seebohm Report, *The Report of the Committee on Local Authority and Allied Personal Social Services*, Cmd. 3703, (HMSO, 1968)

Social Services Inspectors, *For the Children's Sake — A SSI Inspection of Local Authority Adoption Services*, (Department of Health, 1996)

J. Stroud, *An Introduction to the Child Care Service*, (Longmans, 1965)

P. Thane, *The Evolution of the British Welfare State*, (Longman, 1982)

K. Thompson, *The Everyday Lives of Service Users and Social Welfare Workers: A Materialist Analysis*, Ph.d thesis, (James Cook University, 1997)

D. Thorpe, *Evaluating Child Protection*, (Open University Press, 1994)

R. Titmuss, *Problems of Social Policy*, (HMSO and Longmans Green, 1950)

W. Utting, *People Like Us*, (Stationery Office, 1997)

N. Warner, "Tilting at Windmills", *Community Care*, (29 Sept-5 October, 1994)

S. Watson, "The Children's Department and the 1963 Act", in J. Stroud (ed.), *Services for Children and their Families*, (Pergamon Press, 1973)

D. Watkins, *Other People's Children*, (Patten Press, 1993)

E. Weinstein, *The Self-Image of the Foster Child*, (Russell Sage Foundation, 1960)

Williams Report, *Caring for People*, (Allen and Unwin, 1966)

D. Winnicott, *The Child and the Outside World*, (Tavistock Publications, 1957)

D. Winnicott and C. Britton, "Residential management as treatment for difficult children", *Human Relations*, **V**, 1, 1947

E. Younghusband, *Social Work in Britain 1950-1975*, (Allen and Unwin, 1978)